THE UNIVERSITY OF CHICAGO SCHOOL MATHEMATICS PROJECT

Everyday Mathematics

Journal I

Everyday Learning Corporation
Evanston, Illinois

On the Cover: "Zaligs" (Tiles) in New Hassan II Mosque, Morocco.
Photo by Lisl Dennis / Image Bank, Chicago.

Acknowledgements: 2 George Washington Bridge crossing the Hudson River between New York and New Jersey. Photo by Bruce Byers / FPG International, New York.

82 Insect illustrations: Lewis, T. and L. R. Taylor. *Introduction to Experimental Ecology: A Student Guide to Fieldwork and Analysis.* New York: Academic Press Inc., 1967.

ISBN 1-57039-059-2

23456789HS9998979695

Contents

Unit 1: Naming and Constructing Geometric Figures

Unit 2: Using Numbers and Organizing Data

Unit 3: Multiplication and Division; Number Sentences and Algebra

Unit 4:   Decimals and Their Uses

Unit 5:   Map Reference Frames; Measures of Angles

Unit 6: Fractions and Their Uses; Chance and Probability

Activity Sheets

Welcome to *Fourth Grade Everyday Mathematics*

Much of your work in kindergarten through third grade has been basic training in mathematics and its uses. You also spent quite a bit of effort on telling and solving number stories and on learning the basics of arithmetic, including memorizing the basic facts of addition and multiplication.

Fourth Grade Everyday Mathematics builds on this basic training and begins to make the transition to mathematics concepts and ways of using mathematics that are more like what your parents and siblings may have done in high school. We believe, along with many other people, that fourth graders in the 1990's can learn more and do more than was thought to be the case ten or twenty years ago.

Here are some of the things you will be asked to do in *Fourth Grade Everyday Mathematics*:

- Extend your "number sense," "measure sense," and estimation skills.

- Review and extend your skills in the basics of arithmetic—addition, subtraction, multiplication, and division. There isn't much more to learn about the arithmetic of whole numbers, but over the next couple of years you will extend your number skills to being comfortable with the many uses of fractions, percents, and decimals.

- Begin some parts of algebra and the uses of "variables" (letters that hold a place for numbers) that your parents or brothers and sisters may not have encountered until they were in high school.

- Take your geometry skills and concepts somewhat further, with more exact definitions and classifications of geometric figures, with constructions and transformations of figures, and with more work on areas of 2-dimensional figures and volumes of 3-dimensional figures.

- Take a World Tour. Along the way you will consider many kinds of data about various countries and learn about coordinate systems used to locate places on world globes and on flat maps.

- Do many projects involving explorations with numerical data.

As you move beyond your basic training in grades K–3, you will be asked to do more reading and rely on what you can find out for yourself (often working with partners or in groups) rather than being told everything by your teacher.

We hope that you find the activities fun, and that you see some of the real beauty in mathematics. But most important, we hope you become better and better at using mathematics to sort out and solve interesting problems.

Geometry Around Us

Our world is filled with many ideas from geometry—angles, segments, lines, curves, and a great variety of 2-dimensional and 3-dimensional shapes. Many wonderful geometry patterns can be seen in nature—in flowers, spider webs, leaves, sea shells, even in our own faces and bodies.

The ideas of geometry are also found in

the things we create. Think of the games we play. Checkers is played with round pieces on a game board of squares. We play basketball or tennis with a sphere on a rectangular court, painted with straight or curved lines. The next time you play or watch a game, notice how geometry is important to the way the game is played.

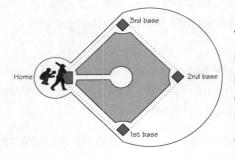

The places we live in are built from plans that use geometry. Buildings have rectangular doors, triangular roofs, curved archways, and straight and spiral staircases. Buildings and the rooms in them are often decorated with beautiful patterns. You see these decorations on doors and windows, on walls, on floors and ceilings, and on railings of staircases.

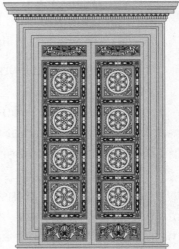

The clothes we wear and the things we use every day are often decorated with geometric shapes.

Things created by ourselves and others throughout history and everywhere in the world often rely on patterns based on geometric shapes. Examples include quilts, pottery, baskets, and tile patterns. Some patterns are shown here. Which are your favorites?

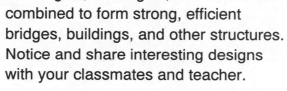

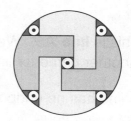

Please make a practice of noticing geometric shapes around you throughout this year. Pay special attention to the ways simple shapes such as triangles, rectangles, and circles are combined to form strong, efficient bridges, buildings, and other structures. Notice and share interesting designs with your classmates and teacher.

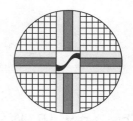

As you continue to study geometric shapes and as you learn to construct them, try to create your own beautiful designs.

Line Segments, Lines, and Rays

This is **line segment AB**. We can write its name as $\overline{AB}$. Another name for line segment AB is line segment BA ($\overline{BA}$).

Points A and B are the **endpoints** of AB.

endpoint   endpoint

A   B

This is **line AB**. We can write its name as $\overleftrightarrow{AB}$. Another name for line AB is line BA ($\overleftrightarrow{BA}$).

A line has no endpoints. It extends infinitely in both directions.

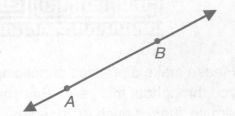

B

A

This is **ray AB**. We can write its name as $\overrightarrow{AB}$. This ray has only one name.

A ray has one endpoint. Starting at its endpoint, it extends infinitely in one direction.

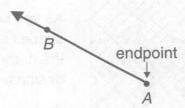

B

endpoint

A

1. List at least 5 things in the classroom that remind you of a line segment.

_____

_____

_____

_____

_____

Use with Lesson 1.

Line Segments, Lines, and Rays (continued)

Use a straightedge to draw the following.

2. Draw and label a line segment TO ($\overline{TO}$).

What is another name for $\overline{TO}$? _____

3. Draw and label a line IF ($\overleftrightarrow{IF}$). Draw a point T on it.

What are two other names for $\overleftrightarrow{IF}$? _____

4. Draw and label a ray ON ($\overrightarrow{ON}$). Draw a point R on it.

What is another name for $\overrightarrow{ON}$? _____

5. Draw a line segment from each point to each of the other points.

• M   • N

• O   • P

a. How many line segments did you draw? _____

b. Write a name for each line segment you drew.

_____

_____

Use with Lesson 1.

Angles

This is **angle ABC**. We can write its name as
∠**ABC**. Another name for angle *ABC* is angle
CBA (∠*CBA*).

An angle has two sides that have the same
endpoint. Here the sides are ray *BA* ($\overrightarrow{BA}$) and
ray *BC* ($\overrightarrow{BC}$). The endpoint is called the **vertex**
of the angle.

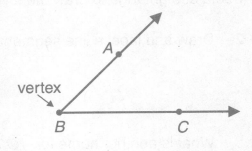

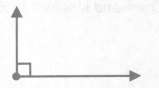

This is a **right angle**. A right angle forms a
square corner.

Use the points shown below to draw angles.

1. Draw angle *AED*. Draw $\overrightarrow{ED}$ and $\overrightarrow{EA}$ through points
    D and *A*. What is the vertex of the angle?   point _____

    What is another name for ∠*AED*?   ∠ _____

2. Draw a right angle whose vertex is point *C*.   It is called ∠ _____ .

3. Draw an angle that is smaller
    than a right angle.   My angle is called ∠ _____ .

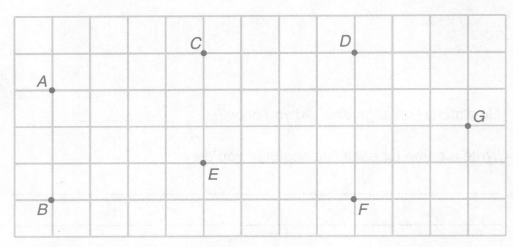

Triangles

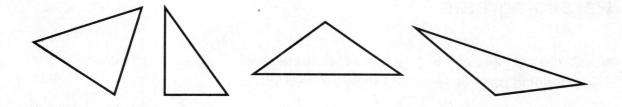

Quadrangles or Quadrilaterals

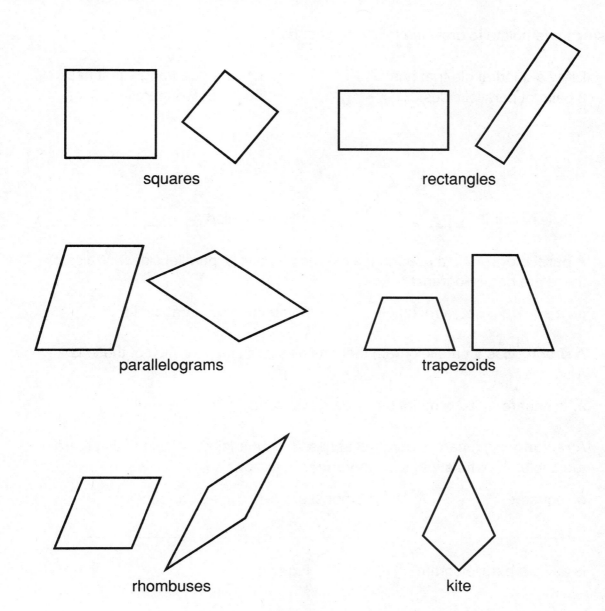

squares

rectangles

parallelograms

trapezoids

rhombuses

kite

Parallelograms

1. Circle the pairs of line segments that are parallel. Test your answers by extending pairs of segments to see if they meet.

   a. _____   **b.**   **c.** 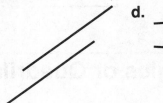   **d.**

Use your template to draw the following shapes.

2. Draw a quadrangle that has 2 pairs of parallel sides.

3. Draw a quadrangle that has only 1 pair of parallel sides.

   This is called a _____.   This is called a _____.

4. A **parallelogram** is a quadrangle that has 2 pairs of parallel sides. Which of these are parallelograms?

   a. a square   **b.** a rectangle   **c.** a rhombus   **d.** a trapezoid

5. A **rhombus** is a parallelogram that has all equal sides. Which of these is a rhombus?

   a. a square   **b.** a rectangle   **c.** a trapezoid

6. A **rectangle** is a parallelogram that has all right angles. Which of these are rectangles? Write **always**, **sometimes**, or **never**.

   a. squares   **b.** rhombuses   **c.** trapezoids

   _____   _____   _____

7. Is a kite a parallelogram? _____ Explain.

   _____

   _____

Convex Polygons

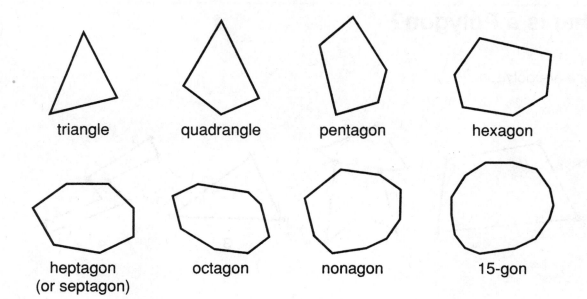

triangle   quadrangle   pentagon   hexagon

heptagon
(or septagon)   octagon   nonagon   15-gon

Concave (nonconvex) Polygons

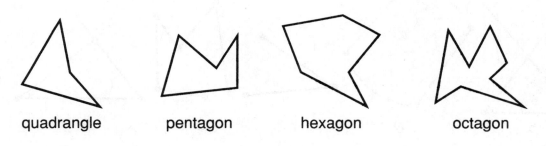

quadrangle   pentagon   hexagon   octagon

Regular Polygons

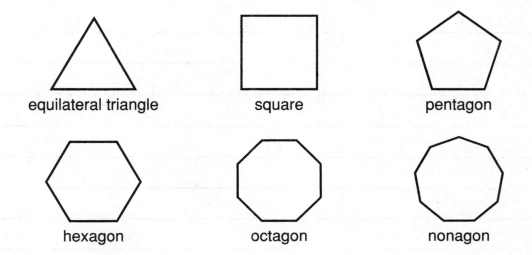

equilateral triangle   square   pentagon

hexagon   octagon   nonagon

Use with Lessons 4 and 5.

What is a Polygon?

These are polygons.

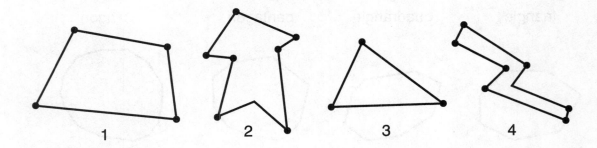

These are not polygons.

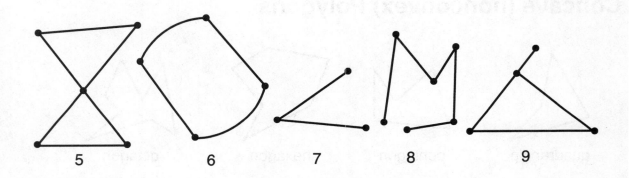

If you had to tell a Martian what a polygon is, what would you say?

_____

_____

_____

_____

_____

_____

_____

_____

Use with Lesson 4.

An Inscribed Square and Regular Octagon

Follow the directions below to make a square.

Step 1: Draw a circle on a sheet of paper. It should be small enough to fit in the top part of the next page. Cut out the circle.

Step 2: With your pencil, make a dot in the center of the circle where the hole is, on both the front and back.

Step 3: Fold the circle in half. Make sure the edges match and the fold line passes through the center.

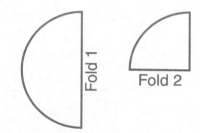

Step 4: Fold it in half again so that the edges match.

Step 5: Unfold your circle. The folds should pass through the center of the circle and form four right angles.

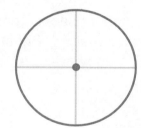

Step 6: Connect the endpoints of the folds with a straightedge to make a square. Cut out the square.

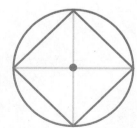

Use your compass to check that the sides of your square are about the same length. If they are, paste or tape the square in the space below.

Challenge

On another sheet of paper, construct a regular octagon. It should be small enough to fit in the space below. Check with your compass that the sides are about the same length. If they are, paste or tape your octagon in the space below.

Circle Constructions

Do each of the constructions on separate sheets of paper. Try and try again until you are satisfied with your work. Then cut out your best construction and paste it in your journal.

1. Use your compass to draw a picture of a circular dart board. Paste your best work in the space below.

The circles in your picture are called **concentric circles**.

A Circle Design

2. **a.** Draw a circle with your compass.

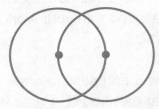

  b. Without changing the opening of
       your compass, draw a second
       circle that passes through the
       center of the first circle.

  c. Without changing the opening of
       your compass, draw a third circle
       that passes through the center of
       each of the first two circles.

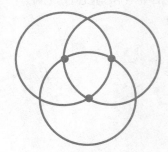

Try and try again until you are satisfied with
your work. Then cut it out and paste it in
the space below.

A Circle Design (continued)

Challenge

3. Try to draw this design with your compass. Work on separate sheets of paper until you are satisfied with your work. Color your best design. Then cut it out and paste it in the space below.

   Hint: Start by making the 3-circle design on page 14. Then add more circles to it.

Use with Lesson 6.

Create your own circle designs.

Date _____ Time _____

Complete the problems. Work as fast as you can. Record your starting time and your ending time.

1. $15 - 8 =$ _____   21. $10 - 2 =$ _____

2. $12 - 5 =$ _____   22. $14 - 8 =$ _____

3. $14 - 9 =$ _____   23. $13 - 5 =$ _____

4. $15 - 6 =$ _____   24. $10 - 4 =$ _____

5. $13 - 9 =$ _____   25. $16 - 9 =$ _____

6. $14 - 6 =$ _____   26. $11 - 3 =$ _____

7. $10 - 3 =$ _____   27. $12 - 6 =$ _____

8. $13 - 6 =$ _____   28. $11 - 7 =$ _____

9. $16 - 7 =$ _____   29. $10 - 6 =$ _____

10. $14 - 5 =$ _____   30. $12 - 3 =$ _____

11. $18 - 9 =$ _____   31. $15 - 9 =$ _____

12. $16 - 8 =$ _____   32. $10 - 7 =$ _____

13. $17 - 9 =$ _____   33. $9 - 9 \ \ =$ _____

14. $10 - 1 =$ _____   34. $12 - 7 =$ _____

15. $11 - 4 =$ _____   35. $11 - 6 =$ _____

16. $12 - 8 =$ _____   36. $14 - 7 =$ _____

17. $15 - 7 =$ _____   37. $13 - 8 =$ _____

18. $11 - 5 =$ _____   38. $12 - 9 =$ _____

19. $12 - 4 =$ _____   39. $4 - 0 \ \ =$ _____

20. $13 - 7 =$ _____   40. $13 - 4 =$ _____

Starting time: _____   Ending time: _____   Time it took: _____

Total Score: _____

Use with Lesson 7.

Hexagons in Our World

The hexagons that you are learning to construct with straightedge and compass are seen in the natural world and in things that people construct and use. For example, honeycombs are made of many hexagonal prisms, and snowflakes suggest the shape of a hexagon.

Soccer balls are made up of regular hexagons and regular pentagons.

All over the world and for many centuries, wonderful tile designs have been created, especially in Islamic art. These often start with hexagon constructions. As these pictures show, a basic hexagon pattern can be developed in many ways for tile designs.

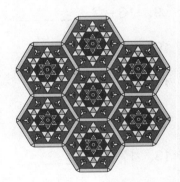

Many quilt and fabric designs come from dividing regular hexagons into triangles or rhombuses (as you may have done with pattern blocks) and coloring them in a variety of ways.

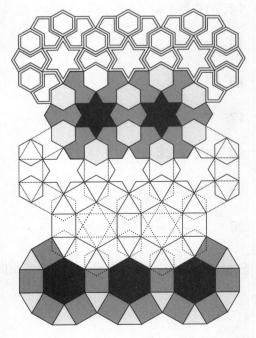

Use with Lesson 7.

Constructing a Regular, Inscribed Hexagon

Step 1: Draw a circle. Keep the same compass opening for Steps 2 and 3. Make a dot on the circle. Place the anchor of your compass on the dot and make a mark with the pencil point on the circle.

Step 2: Place the anchor of your compass on the mark you just made and make another mark with the pencil point on the circle.

Step 3: Do this four more times to divide the circle into 6 equal parts. The 6th mark should be on the dot you started with or very close to it.

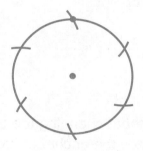

Step 4: With your straightedge, connect the 6 marks **on** the circle to form a regular hexagon.

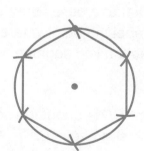

Use your compass to check that the sides of the hexagon are about the same length.

Use with Lesson 7.

Copying a Line Segment

Step 1: Draw line segment *AB*.

A   B

Step 2: Draw a second line segment. It should be longer than $\overline{AB}$. Label one of its endpoints *C*.

C

Step 3: Open your compass so that the anchor is on one endpoint of line segment *AB* and the pencil point is on the other endpoint.

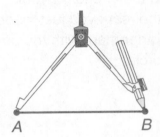

A   B

Step 4: Without changing the compass opening, place the anchor on point *C*. Make a mark that crosses the new line segment. Label the point where the mark crosses the line segment with the letter *D*.

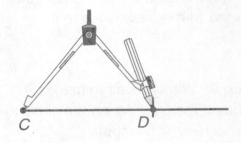

C   D

Line segment *CD* is about the same length as line segment *AB*.

 ## Are You Ready for School?

In the Philippine Islands, a rule of thumb had to be devised to determine when students were old enough to enter school. Instead of sorting students by age, (which was difficult at that time because there were no birth records when universal education was introduced in the Philippines), the teachers found that a child was old enough to send to school when he could cross his arms over his head and grasp his ears with his opposite hands.

Source: Parker, Tom. *Rules of Thumb*. Boston: Houghton Mifflin, 1983.

Use with Lesson 7.

More Constructions

1. Draw a line segment *AN* about the
    same length as segment *GO*. Use
    a compass and straightedge.

    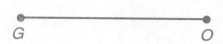

    G   O

2. Construct a regular hexagon on a separate sheet of paper. Try it several times,
    until you are satisfied with your work. Tape or paste your best work in the space
    below.

3. Divide the hexagon into 6 equilateral triangles.

Use with Lesson 7.

6-Point Designs

1. This 6-pointed star is called a **hexagram**. Use your compass and straightedge to construct a hexagram on a separate sheet of paper.

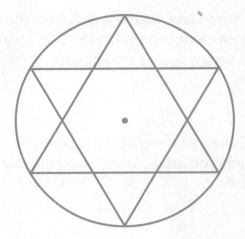

2. Construct a large hexagram. Draw a second hexagram inside the first, then a third hexagram inside the second. Make a hexagram design by coloring your construction.

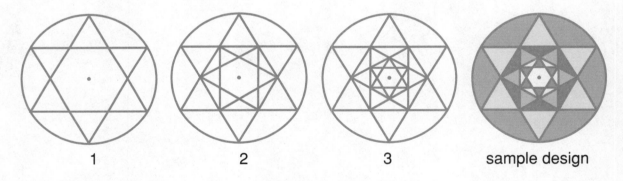

1   2   3   sample design

3. Construct the hexagram pattern several more times. Color each one in a different way to create a new design.

4. Construct this pattern several times. Color each one in a different way.

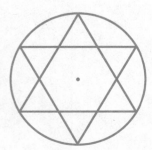

Create your own design.

How to Construct a Kite

Step 1: Draw points *A* and *B*.

A •   • B

Step 2: Set your compass opening so that it is
more than half the distance between *A* and *B*.
Place the point of the compass on point *A* and
draw an arc. Without changing the compass
opening, place the point of the compass on point
B and draw a second arc that intersects the first
one. Label the point where the two arcs meet
point *C*.

A •   • B

C

D

Step 3: Change your compass opening so that it
is still more than half the distance between *A*
and *B*. Repeat Step 2 as shown in the picture
and label the new point of intersection point *D*.

A •   • B

C

Step 4: With your straightedge, connect the
points to form a quadrangle.

D

A   B

C

How would you use this method to construct a rhombus?

_____

_____

_____

The World of Numbers

It is hard to imagine spending just one day without using or thinking about a number. Numbers are almost as much a part of the way we think and communicate as words. But not all numbers are used in the same way.

1) **Numbers can be used for counting.** = To count things

We use the whole numbers 1, 2, 3, ... to count things: Count the number of correct answers on a test or the number of TV programs watched in a week. Some quantities may be so large that no one person could actually count them: For example, the number of people who live in the U.S. Counts are usually exact, but with very large numbers, they may just be estimates.

2) **Numbers can be used for measuring.** = To measure

Measures became a part of your life from the moment you were born: Someone measured and recorded your weight and your length. A long time ago, people discovered that measures often fall between whole numbers, so they invented fractions and decimals to name those "in-between" numbers. Every measurement, no matter how carefully done, is an approximation. Even if we don't say it, we should think of a measurement as an "about" number: For example, the width of this page is about $8\frac{1}{2}$ inches.

3) **Numbers can be used to specify locations in reference frames.** = Show order

Some numbers make sense only if they are thought of in relation to something else, such as: another number, a point on a number line, or even a system of numbers, letters, or words. For example, to understand a temperature reading, you need to think of it in relation to the 0° mark on a thermometer: A temperature of 50°C is either very hot or very cold, depending on whether it is above or below zero. We think of time with relation to noon: 10:00 A.M. or P.M. Graphs may have numbers along their edges (axes) to help us display numerical information. When numbers are used within a reference frame, we may need to use negative numbers: For example, –5°F temperature reading.

Numbers can be used to express ratios.

These are usually pairs of numbers, expressed as fractions, decimals, or percents. You will use such numbers quite a bit from now on.

4) **Numbers can be used as identification numbers and codes.** = to label or identify

Examples of these are product codes to identify things you buy, addresses and phone numbers, locker numbers, and social security numbers.

Numbers that are used to count or measure things or in reference frames always come with a unit: 15 **books**, 7.4 **centimeters**, 15 **degrees** above zero. Numbers that are used to express ratios or identification codes have no unit.

Use with Lesson 9.

Date _____ Time _____

A Visit to Washington, D.C.

Refer to pages 3 and 4 in your *World Tour Book* to answer Questions 1–4.

1. About how many people tour the White House every year? Check off the correct answer.

    ___ between 100 thousand and 1 million   ___ between 1 million and 10 million

    ___ between 10 million and 100 million   ___ between 100 million and 1 billion

2. About how many people rode the Washington Metrorail in 1993? Check off the correct answer.

    ___ between 100 thousand and 1 million   ___ between 1 million and 10 million

    ___ between 10 million and 100 million   ___ between 100 million and 1 billion

3. About how long does it take to add about 50,000 items to the Library of Congress? _____

4. Draw a dot for each of the following events on the time line below. Label the dot with the appropriate letter.

    A The year the Metrorail opened   **B** The year of the flight of the Flyer

    C The year construction started on the Capitol Building   **D** The year the Washington Monument was completed

    E The year the Lincoln Memorial was built   **F** The year of the first nonstop flight across the Atlantic

    G The year the Jefferson Memorial was dedicated   **H** The year of the first landing on the moon

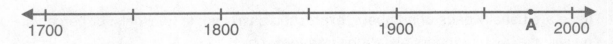

1700   1800   1900   **A** 2000

5. Use your map of North America on pages 30 and 31 in your *World Tour Book*. Find at least one city or town that is about as far from Washington, D.C. as the total length of the bookshelves in the Library of Congress.

Name-Collection Boxes

1. Write 10 names in each box. Use as many different kinds of numbers and operations as you can.

2. Put your own number on the tag and fill up the box.

a.

24

b.

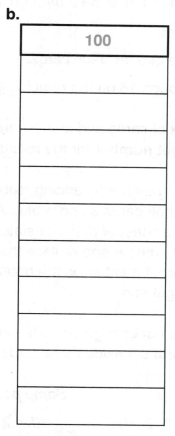

100

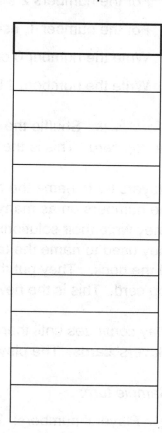

💡 A Googol

The mathematician Edward Kasner once asked his 9-year-old son to invent a name for a very large number. The number consisted of a 1 followed by 100 zeros. The boy named this large number a "googol." A short way to write a googol is 10^{100}; it is read as "10 to the 100th power." Mathematicians have used the name "googol" ever since.

Kasner's nephew later named an even larger number. He called it a "googolplex." A googolplex consists of a 1 followed by a googol of zeros—10 to the googol power. It is written as $10^{10^{100}}$.

Use with Lesson 10.

Name That Number

This game is for 2 or 3 players.

Materials: Make up a deck of number cards from an ordinary deck of playing cards, as follows:

- For the numbers 2 through 10, use the 2 through 10 cards.
- For the number 1, use aces.
- Write the number 0 on the queens' face cards.
- Write the numbers 11 through 18 on the remaining face cards (kings, jacks).

Directions: Shuffle the deck of cards and deal 5 cards to each player. Turn over the top card. This is the **target number** for the round.

Players try to name the target number by adding, subtracting, multiplying, or dividing the numbers on as many of their cards as possible. A card can only be used once. They write their solutions on a sheet of paper or slate. Then they set aside the cards they used to name the target number and replace them with new cards from the top of the deck. They put the target number on the bottom of the deck and turn over the top card. This is the new target number.

Play continues until there are not enough cards left in the deck to replace both players' cards. The player who set aside more cards wins the game.

Sample turn:

Players' numbers: 7 5 8 2 10

Target number: 16

Some possible solutions:

$$7 \times 2 = 14 \rightarrow 14 + \mathbf{10} = 24$$
$$\rightarrow 24 - \mathbf{8} = 16$$
(four cards used)

$$8 \div 2 = 4 \rightarrow 4 + \mathbf{10} = 14$$
$$\rightarrow 14 + \mathbf{7} = 21$$
$$\rightarrow 21 - \mathbf{5} = 16$$
(all five cards used)

Date _____ Time _____

Math Boxes

---

1. Fill in the blanks.

20 dimes = $_____._____

20 nickels = $_____._____

20 quarters = $_____._____

10 quarters
and 7 dimes = $_____._____

---

2. Put these numbers in order from smallest to largest.

2080   2008   2800   2088   20,800

_____ _____ _____ _____ _____

---

3. Draw a rectangular array of 36 X's with 6 X's in each row. How many rows are there?

_____ rows

---

4. Name this regular polygon.

_____

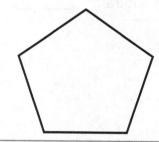

---

5. Draw a parallelogram. Label the vertices so that side *AB* is parallel to side *CD*.

Methods for Addition

There are all kinds of ways to add numbers. You may have discovered several methods yourself. One way is to change the addends so that one of them ends in zero. To do this, you can use the following rule:

Opposite-Change Rule

In an addition problem, if you add a number to one addend and subtract the same number from the other addend, the sum in the new problem is the same as the sum in the problem you started with. For example:

Add and subtract 1:	Subtract and add 3:	Add and subtract 5:
$79 \rightarrow 80$	$79 \rightarrow 76$	$185 \rightarrow 190$
$+\ 47 \rightarrow +\ 46$	$+\ 47 \rightarrow +\ 50$	$+\ 76 \rightarrow +\ 71$
126	126	261

Try a few problems the new way. Fill in the blanks.

1. Add and subtract _____.

	5	8	→		
+	3	5	→		

2. Add and subtract _____.

	8	6	→		
+	6	6	→		

3. Add and subtract _____.

	2	2	7	→		
+		8	3	→		

4. Add and subtract _____.

	1	5	9	→		
+		6	4	→		

Try to do these in your head.

5. Add and subtract _____.

$18 + 66 =$ _____

6. Add and subtract _____.

_____ $= 21 + 59$

Methods For Addition (continued)

Here is another method for adding numbers. You add from left to right, one column at a time. When adding in this way, always keep in mind what number each digit stands for. In the example below, think "700 + 400 = 1100," not "7 + 4 = 11."

Partial Sums Method:

	7	6	8
+	4	8	3
1	1	0	0
	1	4	0
		1	1
1	2	5	1

Add the hundreds: 700 + 400 →

Add the tens: 60 + 80 →   (1100 + 140 = 1240)

Add the ones: 8 + 3 →   (1240 + 11 = 1251)

Find the total: 1100 + 140 + 11 =

Solve Problems 7–9 using this method and Problems 10–12 by any method you choose. Show your work.

7. 746 + 238 = _____

8. _____ = 647 + 936

9. _____ = 1672 + 3231

10. 196 + 58 = _____

11. _____ = 6586 + 645

12. 17,854 + 24,550 = _____

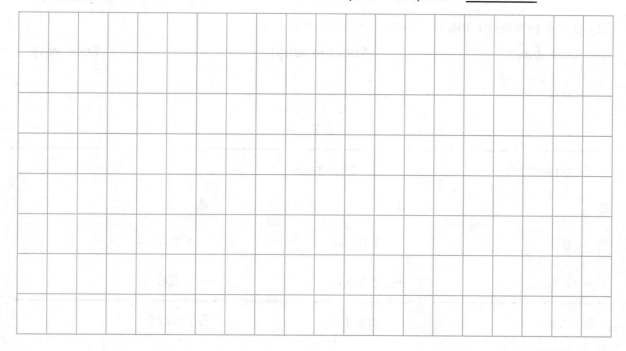

Date _____ Time _____

Methods for Subtraction

You have found that it is possible to change an addition problem to an easier problem by changing **either of the addends** to a number that ends in zero. You can also change subtraction problems to easier problems. But in subtraction, it is best to change the **second number** in the problem to a number that ends in zero—not the first number. Also, the rule for changing subtraction problems is different from the rule for addition.

Same-change Rule for Subtraction

In a subtraction problem, if you **add** the same number to **both** numbers in the problem, the answer to the new problem is the same as the answer to the problem you started with. This will also work if you **subtract** the same number from both numbers in the problem. For example:

One way: Add 2.

$$
\begin{array}{r}
9\,3 \\
-\,5\,8 \\
\end{array}
\rightarrow
\begin{array}{r}
9\,5 \\
-\,6\,0 \\
\hline
\end{array}
$$

Subtract: *35*

Another way: Subtract 8.

$$
\begin{array}{r}
9\,3 \\
-\,5\,8 \\
\end{array}
\rightarrow
\begin{array}{r}
8\,5 \\
-\,5\,0 \\
\hline
\end{array}
$$

Subtract: *35*

Do you know another way to do the problem? Try it.

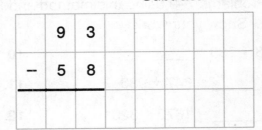

Try a few problems the new way. Fill in the blanks.

1. One way:

$$
\begin{array}{r}
5\,6 \rightarrow \\
-\,2\,7 \rightarrow \\
\hline
\end{array}
$$

Subtract:

Another way:

$$
\begin{array}{r}
5\,6 \rightarrow \\
-\,2\,7 \rightarrow \\
\hline
\end{array}
$$

Subtract:

Your way:

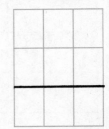

2.

$$
\begin{array}{r}
8\,7 \rightarrow \\
-\,4\,9 \rightarrow \\
\hline
\end{array}
$$

Subtract:

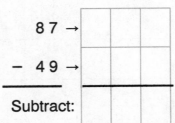

3.

$$
\begin{array}{r}
7\,0 \rightarrow \\
-\,3\,8 \rightarrow \\
\hline
\end{array}
$$

Subtract:

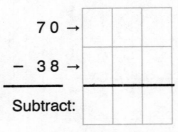

4.

$$
\begin{array}{r}
1\,2\,4 \rightarrow \\
-\,5\,6 \rightarrow \\
\hline
\end{array}
$$

Subtract:

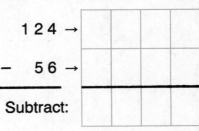

Use with Lesson 13.

Methods for Subtraction (continued)

Here is another method for subtracting numbers. Subtract from left to right, subtracting one column at a time.

Always subtract the smaller number from the larger number.
- If the smaller number is on the bottom, the difference is **added** to the answer.
- If the smaller number is on top, the difference is **subtracted** from the answer.

Partial Differences Method:

	5	2	8
−	2	6	3
	3	0	0
	−	4	0
		+	5
	2	6	5

Subtract the hundreds: 500 − 200 →

Subtract the tens: 60 − 20 →
(smaller number on top)   (300 − 40 = 260)

Subtract the ones: 8 − 3 →   (260 + 5 = 265)

Find the total: 300 − 40 + 5 =

Solve Problems 5–7 using this method and Problems 8–10 by any method you choose. Show your work.

5. 826 − 319 = _____

6. _____ = 942 − 487

7. _____ = 7584 − 2301

8. 609 − 264 = _____

9. _____ = 400 − 271

10. 4601 − 1681 = _____

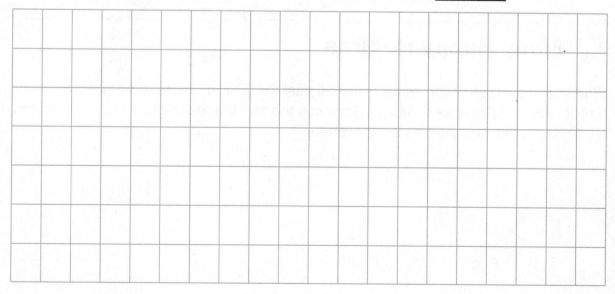

Date _____ Time _____

Math Boxes

---

1. Write the largest number you can make with the following digits.

3   0   3   8   0

___ ___ ___ ___ ___

2. You had $3.28. You spent $1.86 on a magazine. How much money do you have left?

$_____._____

Number model:

_____

3. Make 100's.

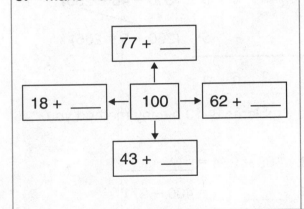

4. Draw a quadrangle that has 2 pairs of parallel sides and no right angles. What kind of quadrangle is this?

_____

💡 Many Happy Returns

With the population of the world now well past the 5 billion mark, a simple division of 5 billion by 366 possible birthdays discloses the fact that each of us probably shares a birthday with more than 13 million others.

Number Lines

Fill in the missing numbers on the number lines. To find the missing numbers:

Step 1: Subtract the first number from the last number on the number line.

Step 2: Count the number of intervals (1 less than the number of marks on the line).

Step 3: Divide the answer to Step 1 by the answer to Step 2. This is the number to count by.

1.

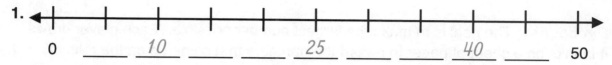

0 _____ *10* _____ _____ *25* _____ _____ _____ *40* _____ 50

2.

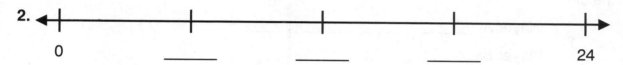

0 _____ _____ _____ 24

3.

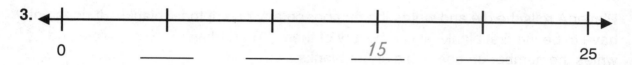

0 _____ _____ *15* _____ 25

4.

0 _____ _____ 18

5.

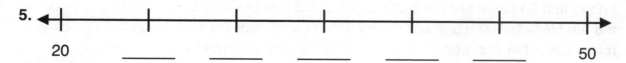

20 _____ _____ _____ _____ 50

6.

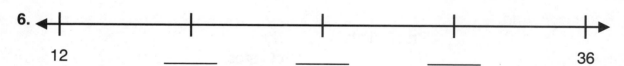

12 _____ _____ _____ 36

7.

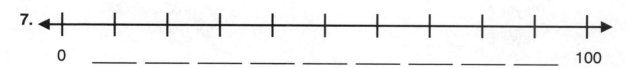

0 _____ _____ _____ _____ _____ _____ _____ _____ _____ 100

8.

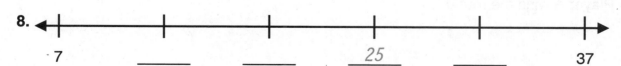

·7 _____ _____ *25* _____ 37

9.

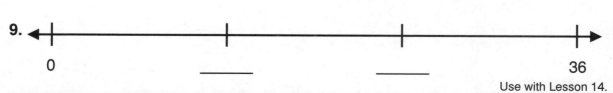

0 _____ _____ 36

Use with Lesson 14.

High-Number Toss

Hundred Millions	Ten Millions	Millions	Hundred Thousands	Ten Thousands	Thousands	Hundreds	Tens	Ones
100M	10M	M	100K	10K	K	H	T	U

Materials: a regular die (6-sided)

If you don't have a die, you can use a deck of playing cards consisting of the aces and the numbers 2 through 6. Instead of rolling the die, you can draw the top card from the deck.

Directions: The goal is to make the largest number possible. Each player draws 4 blanks on a sheet of paper to record the numbers that come up on the rolls of the die:

Player A: _____ _____ _____ | _____

Player B: _____ _____ _____ | _____

Player A rolls the die and writes the number on any one of the 4 blanks. It does not have to be the first blank—it can be any of them. Then Player B rolls the die and writes the number on one of his or her blanks.

Players take turns doing this 3 more times.

Each player then uses the 4 numbers on the blanks to build a number. The numbers on the first 3 blanks are the first 3 digits of the number they build. The number on the 4th blank tells the number of zeros that come after the first 3 digits. Each player reads his or her number. The player with the larger number wins.

Sample Round:

	First 3 digits			Number of zeros		
Player A:	1	3	2	6	=	132,000,000
Player B:	3	5	6	4	=	3,560,000

Player A wins the round.

Math Boxes

1. Write the smallest whole number that you can using all of the following digits. The zero can not be the first digit. 9 2 0 3 1 ____ ____ ____ ____ ____	**2.** Three friends cut a pizza into 12 slices. They shared them equally. What fraction of the pizza did each one get? _____ How many slices did each one get? _____
3. A rock collector had 136 rocks in her collection. She took them to a geologist who said that 57 of them were not valuable. How many of them were valuable? _____ Number model: _____	**4.** 2 quarters = ____ dimes 1 dollar and 5 nickels = ____ quarters 14 dimes = ____ pennies Make up your own. _____ = _____

☀ Sheep

Australia and New Zealand have many times more sheep than people.

	People	Sheep
Australia	13,339,000	145,304,000
New Zealand	2,726,000	55,883,000
Mongolia	1,403,000	14,077,000
Uruguay	3,028,000	15,373,000
Namibia	692,000	4,400,000

Source: Wallechinsky, David, Irving Wallace, and Amy Wallace. *The Book of Lists.* New York: Bantam Books, 1977.

Counting Raisins

1. Use your $\frac{1}{2}$-ounce box of raisins. Do each step when the teacher tells you to.

   a. Don't open your box yet. **Guess** about how
      many raisins are in the box. (Stop)   about _____

   b. Open the box. Count the number of raisins
      in the top layer. Then **estimate** the total
      number of raisins in the box. (Stop)   about _____

   c. Now count the raisins in the box. (Stop)   How many? _____

Work with a partner.

2. Use the data for the whole class. Organize the data in the space below.

3. Find the following landmarks for the class data.

   a. What is the maximum, or largest number of raisins found?   _____

   b. What is the minimum, or smallest number of raisins found?   _____

   c. What is the range? (Subtract the minimum from the maximum.) _____

   d. What is the mode, or most frequent number of raisins?   _____

Use with Lesson 15.

Date _____ Time _____

Math Boxes

---

1. You can use your calculator to solve this problem. Show how you figured it out.

How many minutes are in one day?

_____ minutes

2. Look at the number 42,018.

The 2 stands for ____*2000*____ .

The 1 stands for _____ .

The 8 stands for _____ .

The 4 stands for _____ .

---

3. You went to the store with a $20 bill. Your groceries cost $14.52. How much change should you get?

$_____._____

How could you get this with the fewest number of bills and coins?

_____

_____

---

4. Gina's parents give her a $7 allowance each week if she does her chores. When she forgets to do her chores, she doesn't get an allowance. Instead, she must give her parents $3. During the month of February, Gina remembered to do her chores 2 weeks and forgot to do her chores 2 weeks. How much allowance money did she get in February?

$_____._____

Family Size

Do each step when the teacher tells you to.

1. How many people are in your family? _____ Write it on a sticky note.

2. Make a line plot of the family-size data for the class. Use X's in place of sticky notes.

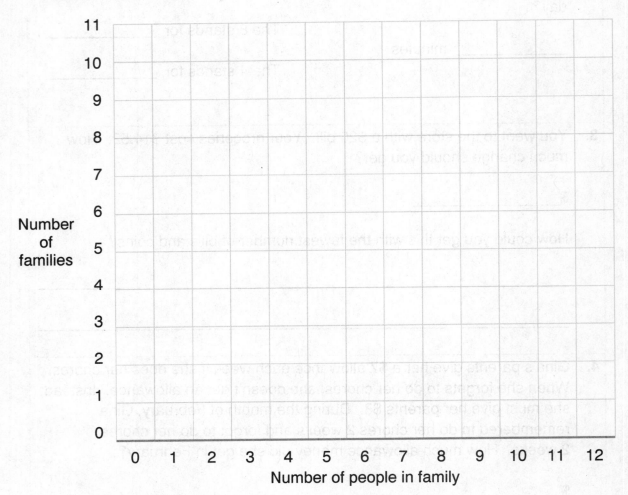

Number of families (vertical axis, 0 to 11)

Number of people in family (horizontal axis, 0 to 12)

3. Find the following landmarks for the class data.

    a. What is the maximum (largest) number of people in a family? _____

    b. What is the minimum (smallest) number of people in a family? _____

    c. What is the range? (Subtract the minimum from the maximum.) _____

    d. What is the mode (most frequent) family size? _____

4. What is the median family size for the class? _____ people

Math Boxes

1.

88 minutes is the same as

_____ hour and _____ minutes.

62 hours is the same as

_____ days and _____ hours.

---

2. Lisa's marble collection contains 287 marbles. 67 of them are white. 59 of them are blue. 74 are green. The rest are multicolored. How many are multicolored? Show how you figured it out.

_____ multicolored marbles

---

3. Put these numbers in order from smallest to largest.

16,000   10,006   10,060   10,600

_____, _____, _____, _____

---

4. Use your calculator. Write the answers in dollars and cents.

64¢ + $1.73 = $_____._____

$0.85 + 53¢ = $_____._____

$2.01 + $5.01 = $_____._____

37¢ + 26¢ = $_____._____

The Size of Your Head

Your body is about 8 times the height of your head; your shoulders are about twice the width of your head; and your foot is about equal to the height of your head.

Source: Parker, Tom. *Rules of Thumb*. Boston: Houghton Mifflin, 1983.

Hat Sizes

Ms. Woods owns a clothing store. She is trying to decide how many children's hats to stock in each possible size. Should she stock the same number of hats in each size? Or should she stock more hats in the more popular hat sizes?

To help her decide, pretend that she has asked each class in your school to collect and organize data about the students' head sizes. She plans to combine the data for all the classes and use the data to figure out how many hats of each size to stock.

Work with the rest of your class to collect and organize data about each others' head sizes.

1. Ask your partner to help you measure the distance around your head.

    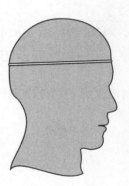

    - Wind a piece of string around your head.

    - Mark the length and cut off the extra string.

    - Measure the string to the nearest $\frac{1}{2}$-centimeter.

    - Keep the string.

    Your head size: about _____ cm

2. What is the median head size for the class?   about _____ cm

---

 ## What's Your Hat Size?

The hat sizes of men and women in stores are not recorded in the same way. A woman's hat size is the distance around the head in inches. To understand a man's hat size, you have to imagine taking the inside band of a man's hat and pushing it into a circle. The size of the hat is the diameter of this circle in inches.

Men's hat sizes are measured this way because until about 1800, newly-made hats were perfectly round. Men had to use special devices, called hat screws, to force their hats into a more comfortable oval shape to fit their heads.

Hat Sizes (continued)

3. Make a bar graph of the head-size data for the class.

4. For the cap used by your group, measure—

   a. The smallest size to the nearest
      $\frac{1}{2}$-centimeter.   about _____ cm

   b. The largest size.   about _____ cm

5. Compare these measurements to the data in
   the bar graph. Could this hat be adjusted to fit
   anyone in your class?   _____

Use with Lesson 17.

Multiplication/Division Facts Table

*, /	1	2	3	4	5	6	7	8	9	10
1	1	2	3	4	5	6	7	8	9	10
2	2	4	6	8	10	12	14	16	18	20
3	3	6	9	12	15	18	21	24	27	30
4	4	8	12	16	20	24	28	32	36	40
5	5	10	15	20	25	30	35	40	45	50
6	6	12	18	24	30	36	42	48	54	60
7	7	14	21	28	35	42	49	56	63	70
8	8	16	24	32	40	48	56	64	72	80
9	9	18	27	36	45	54	63	72	81	90
10	10	20	30	40	50	60	70	80	90	100

Use with Lesson 19 and after.

Math Boxes

1. Solve.

   a. 459 + 291 = _____   **b.** _____ = 389 + 712

   c. _____ = 120 + 880   **d.** 72 + 63 = _____

2. Target number: 15
   Numbers: 12, 3, 8, 15, 4
   Try to name the target number using all four operations and as many of the given numbers as possible. Show your solution.

   _____

3. The ages of Maria's cousins are: 3, 4, 15, 1, 4, and 12 years.

   What is the median age of her cousins? _____ years

   What is the mode? _____ years

Use with Lesson 19.

Rules for *Baseball Multiplication*

Beginners' Game:

Materials:
2 regular dice
4 pennies
a Multiplication Table or a calculator

Number of players:

Directions:
Take turns being the "pitcher" and the "batter."

1. At the start of the inning, the batter puts a penny on home plate.

2. The pitcher rolls the 2 dice. The batter multiplies the 2 numbers that come up and tells the answer. The pitcher checks the answer in a multiplication table or on a calculator.

3. The batter looks up the product in the **Hitting Table** on page 47. If it is a hit, the batter moves all pennies on base as follows:

Single	1 base
Double	2 bases
Triple	3 bases
Home Run	4 bases or across home plate

4. A run is scored each time a penny crosses home plate. If a play is not a hit, it is an out.

5. A player remains the batter for 3 outs. Then players switch roles. The inning is over when both players have made 3 outs.

6. After making the third out, a batter records the number of runs scored in that inning on the Scoreboard.

7. The player who has more runs at the end of 4 innings wins the game. If the game is tied at the end of 4 innings, play continues into extra innings until one player wins.

8. If, at the end of the first half of the last inning, the second player is ahead, there is no need to play the second half of the inning. The player who is ahead wins.

Use with Lesson 20.

Baseball Multiplication Playing Mat

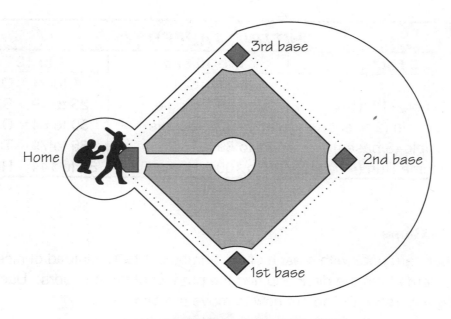

HITTING TABLE	
1 to 6 Facts	
1 to 9	Out
10 to 19	Single (1 base)
20 to 29	Double (2 bases)
30 to 35	Triple (3 bases)
36	Home Run (4 bases)

Make your own Scoreboards, like the one below, on a separate sheet of paper.

SAMPLE SCOREBOARD						Extra Innings			
Inning		1	2	3	4	5	6	7	Final Score
Team: *The Eagles*	outs	|||	|||	|||	|||	|||			
	runs	1	0	2	1	1			5
Team: *The Knights*	outs	|||	|||	|||	|||	|||			
	runs	0	3	1	0	0			4

SCOREBOARD						Extra Innings			
Inning		1	2	3	4	5	6	7	Final Score
Team:	outs								
	runs								
Team:	outs								
	runs								

Use with Lesson 20.

Rules for *Baseball Multiplication* (continued)

HITTING TABLES		
1 to 6 Facts	**1 to 10 Facts**	**1 to 12 Facts**
1 to 9 Out	1 to 21 Out	1 to 24 Out
10 to 19 Single (1 base)	22 to 45 Single	25 to 49 Single
20 to 29 Double (2 bases)	46 to 70 Double	50 to 64 Double
30 to 35 Triple (3 bases)	71 to 89 Triple	65 to 79 Triple
36 Home Run (4 bases)	90 to 100 Home Run	80 to 144 Home Run

1 to 10 Facts Game

Use a number card deck with 4 each of the numbers 1 to 10 instead of dice. At each turn, draw 2 cards from the deck and find the product of the numbers. Use the **1 to 10 Facts Hitting Table** to find out how to move the pennies.

1 to 12 Facts Game

At each turn, roll 4 regular dice. Separate them into 2 pairs. Add the numbers in each pair and multiply the sums.

For example, suppose you roll a 2, 3, 5, and 6. You could separate them as follows:

$2 + 3 = 5$	$2 + 5 = 7$	$2 + 6 = 8$
$5 + 6 = 11$	$3 + 6 = 9$	$3 + 5 = 8$
$5 * 11 = 55$	$7 * 9 = 63$	$8 * 8 = 64$

How you pair the numbers can make a difference in the kind of hit or out.

World Series

Choose 2 teams of players as in real baseball. Make up a batting order. The first team to win 4 games wins the World Series.

For a shorter Series, play the best 3 out of 5 games.

Use with Lesson 21.

Math Boxes

1. Write 5 names for the number 34. Use as many different kinds of numbers and operations as you can.

a. _____

b. _____

c. _____

d. _____

e. _____

2. Build a numeral. Write:
- 6 in the hundreds place
- 0 in the millions place
- 2 in the tens place
- 8 in the hundred thousands
- 5 in the ones place
- 3 in the thousands place
- 4 in the ten thousands place

Answer: _____   Read your answer to someone.

3. Continue the pattern.

1,
10,
100,

_____,

_____,

_____

4. You went to the store with a $10 bill and a $5 bill. Your groceries cost $11.77. How much change should you get?

$_____. _____

Multiplication Top-It

Materials: 1 deck of number cards 1–10 (4 of each for a total of 40 cards)

Number of players: 2 to 4

Directions: Each player turns over 2 cards and calls out the product of the 2 numbers.

The player with the highest product takes all the cards. In case of a tie for the highest product, each tied player turns over 2 more cards and calls out the product. The player with the highest product takes all the cards from both plays.

Sample round:	Player A draws a 6 and 4.	6 * 4 = 24
	Player B draws a 3 and 8.	3 * 8 = 24
	Player C draws a 7 and 2.	7 * 2 = 14

Players A and B are tied with the highest product. They both turn over 2 more cards.

| | Player A draws a 9 and 4. | 9 * 4 = 36 |
| | Player B draws a 7 and 6. | 7 * 6 = 42 |

Player B has the higher product and takes all the cards.

Answers can be checked in a Multiplication Table or on a calculator.

Play continues until there are too few cards left for each player to have another turn. The player who took the most cards wins.

Beat the Calculator

Materials: 1 deck of number cards 1–10 (4 of each for a total of 40 cards)
calculator

Number of players: 3

Directions: One player is the "caller," a second player is the "calculator," and the third is the "brain."

Shuffle the deck of cards and place it face down on the playing surface.

The caller turns over the top two cards from the deck. These are the factors. The calculator finds the product with a calculator, while the brain solves it without a calculator. The caller decides who got the answer first.

Players trade roles every 10 turns or so.

Use with Lesson 21.

Math Boxes

---

1. What is the value of the digit **8** in the numbers below?

    a. 584   _____ *80* _____

    b. 38,067   _____

    c. 49,841   _____

    d. 820,731   _____

---

2. Solve.

    a. _____ $= 72 - 35$ **b.** _____ $= 489 - 95$

    c. $503 - 121 =$ _____   **d.** $830 - 342 =$ _____

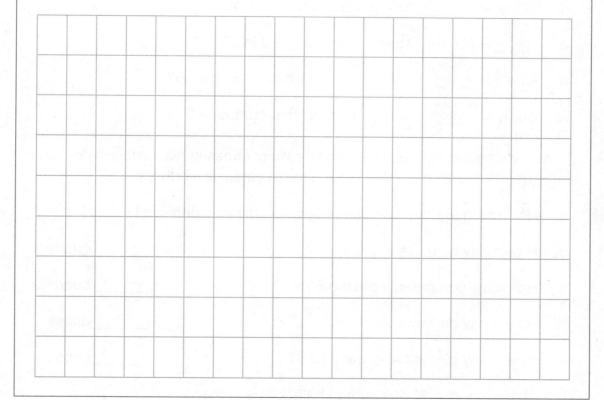

Multiplication and Division

Symbols		
3 * 4 3 × 4	12/3 12 ÷ 3 $\frac{12}{3}$ 3)12	3 < 5 5 > 3

1. Choose 3 Fact Triangles. Write the fact family for each.

_____ * _____ = _____ | _____ × _____ = _____ | _____ * _____ = _____

_____ * _____ = _____ | _____ × _____ = _____ | _____ * _____ = _____

_____ / _____ = _____ | _____ / _____ = _____ | _____ ÷ _____ = _____

_____ / _____ = _____ | _____ / _____ = _____ | _____ ÷ _____ = _____

2. Solve each division fact.

a. 27 / 3 = _____   Think: How many 3's in 27?

b. _____ = 45 / 5   Think: How many 5's in 45?

c. 36 ÷ 6 = _____   Think: 6 times what number = 36?

d. 24 / 8 = _____   Think: 8 times what number = 24?

3. A cashier has 5 rolls of quarters and 6 rolls of dimes in his cash register. Each roll of quarters is worth $10 and each roll of dimes is worth $5.

a. How much are the rolls of quarters and dimes worth in all? $ _____

b. How many quarters are in 1 roll?   _____ quarters

c. How many quarters are in the 5 rolls?   _____ quarters

d. How many dimes are in 1 roll?   _____ dimes

e. How many dimes are in the 6 rolls?   _____ dimes

f. There are also $7.50 worth of half-dollars in the cash register. That's how many half-dollars?   _____ half-dollars

Use with Lesson 22.

Math Boxes

1. Following is a table giving the number of books a group of fourth graders read during the summer months. Draw a graph below from the data given.

Sally	Jon	Marcus	Liz	Ishmel	Freddie	Monica	Carl
15	21	29	10	25	18	9	12

What was the median number of books
read by this group of students?   _____

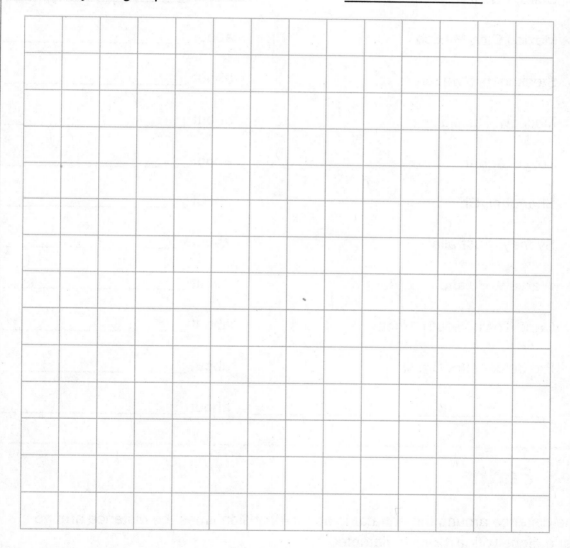

Date _____ Time _____

Measuring Air Distance

Which city listed below is the closest to Washington, D.C.? _____

Which is the farthest? _____

Air distance from Washington, D.C. to:

Cairo, Egypt   about _____

Mexico City, Mexico   about _____

Stockholm, Sweden   about _____

Moscow, Russia   about _____

Tokyo, Japan   about _____

Shanghai, China   about _____

Sydney, Australia   about _____

Warsaw, Poland   about _____

Cape Town, South Africa   about _____

Rio de Janeiro, Brazil   about _____

_____   about _____

Earth

The distance around the equator is about 42 million times the distance around a world globe with a 12-inch diameter.

If the earth were a huge, empty ball, it would be possible to fill it with about 50,000,000,000,000,000,000,000 twelve-inch world globes. This number is read as "50 sextillion." Another way to write this number is 5×10^{22}. This is read as "5 times 10 to the 22nd power."

Use with Lesson 24.

Math Boxes

1. Fill in the missing numbers on the number lines.

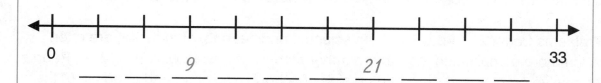

0   _____ _____ *9* _____ _____ _____ _____ *21* _____ _____ _____   33

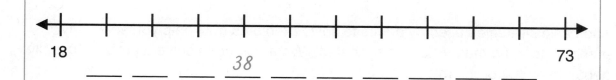

18   _____ _____ _____ *38* _____ _____ _____ _____ _____ _____ _____   73

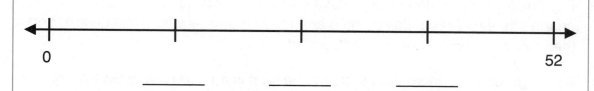

0   _____   _____   _____   52

2. Use your calculator to complete the following problem.

- Enter 306,139.

- Use the [−] key to change the digit in the hundreds place to a 7.

- Use the [+] key to change the digit in the ten thousands to an 8.

What is your new number?   _____

Record your keystrokes to show what you entered on your calculator.

_____

_____

_____

_____

Solving Number Stories

You have been solving number stories ever since you started school. In fact, you probably solved number stories even before that—but you may not have been aware of it. As you became older, the number stories became a little more complicated— but that was O.K. because your math skills were getting better and better.

Problems from day-to-day life, from science, engineering, or industry, are often much more complicated than the "number stories" you work with in school. People who solve problems in the world outside of school use some, and often all, of the strategies shown in the diagram on the next page.

The basic strategies used by adults to solve problems may help you solve any number story, no matter how complicated. What you do to solve a problem usually depends on the problem.

- For simple number stories, you may be able to go directly from reading or hearing the problem to doing some arithmetic (perhaps with a calculator), and then recording an answer (a number and a unit).

- If the problem has more data than you need, it is a good idea to list the data and experiment with it, until you know exactly what data you do need. When doing this, you may even find out that the problem does not have all the data you need to solve it.

- Sometimes you may list all the data you have first, identify what you want to find out, and then return to the data.

- At other times, you may try to make clear what the problem is all about, and then figure out what data you need to solve the problem.

- It is often helpful to act out the problem with the help of objects, such as counting chips, by making pictures of what is going on, by filling in tables or diagrams, or with whatever else may help you. Scientists, engineers, and other adults often do this, and you should too! People who go straight to doing the arithmetic are usually not the better problem solvers.

Whatever else you do, always go back to the problem to check whether your answer makes sense. If you need to, "go back to the drawing board": Check your arithmetic, look at the data again, even review the problem to see whether the question you are trying to answer is the right question.

Date _____ Time _____

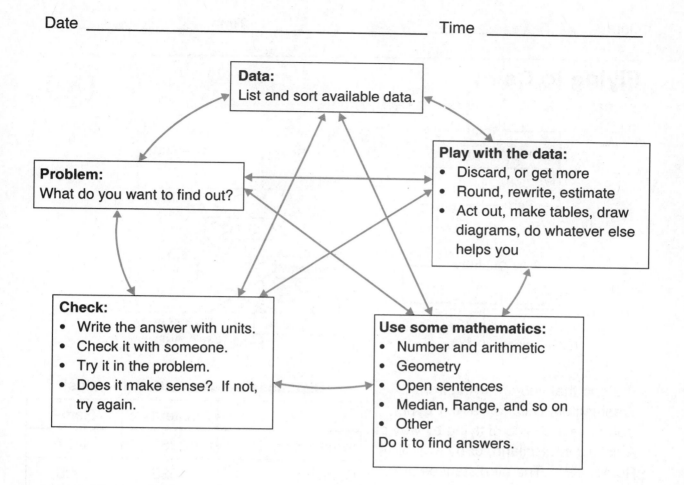

Data:
List and sort available data.

Play with the data:
- Discard, or get more
- Round, rewrite, estimate
- Act out, make tables, draw diagrams, do whatever else helps you

Problem:
What do you want to find out?

Check:
- Write the answer with units.
- Check it with someone.
- Try it in the problem.
- Does it make sense? If not, try again.

Use some mathematics:
- Number and arithmetic
- Geometry
- Open sentences
- Median, Range, and so on
- Other
Do it to find answers.

Think about how to solve the following problem. It will be discussed in detail at the beginning of class, so don't worry if you find it difficult to solve.

The Great Pyramid and the St. Louis Arch

The *Great Pyramid of Egypt* is on the outskirts of Cairo. Completed about 2580 B.C., it is one of the *Seven Wonders of the Ancient World*. Its original height was a little over 146 meters. Over the years, its height has been reduced by a little over 9 meters. It took about 100,000 slaves about 30 years to build it. They used about $2\frac{1}{2}$ million limestone blocks, whose total weight was about 6,400,000 tons.

The Great Pyramid is not the tallest monument in the world. The record belongs to the *Gateway to the West Arch* in St. Louis, Missouri. The arch was completed in 1965 and stands about 192 meters tall.

How much taller is the Gateway Arch than the Great Pyramid?

about _____ meters

Use with Lesson 25.

Flying to Cairo

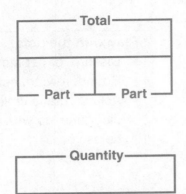

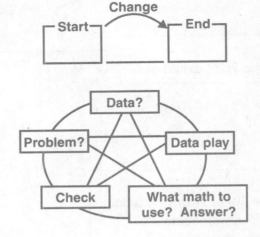

Pretend that you are flying from Washington, D.C. to Cairo, Egypt. You have a choice of flying by way of Amsterdam, Holland, or by way of Rome, Italy. The air distances are shown in the table at the right.

Distances between cities (in miles)

	Amsterdam	Rome
Washington, D.C.	3851	4497
Cairo	2035	1326

If you fly first class, your ticket will cost $850. If you fly economy class, you will save $175.

1. About how many more miles is it from Washington to Rome than from Washington to Amsterdam?

   _____
   (number model)

   Answer: about _____ miles

2. What is the total distance from Washington to Cairo by way of Amsterdam?

   _____
   (number model)

   Answer: about _____ miles

Flying to Cairo (continued)

3. What is the total distance from Washington to Cairo by way of Rome?

   _____
   (number model)

   Answer: about _____ miles

4. About how many fewer miles will you fly, if you go by way of Rome?

   _____
   (number model)

   Answer: about _____ fewer miles

5. How much will your ticket cost if you fly economy class?

   _____
   (number model)

   Answer: $ _____

6. One of the flights to Amsterdam leaves Washington at 1:15 P.M. It lands in Amsterdam 8 hours and 45 minutes later.

   a. At what time does it land, Washington time?

      Answer: _____ (A.M. or P.M.?)

   b. At what time does it land, Amsterdam time? (Use the Time Zones map on page 17 of your *World Tour Book*.)

      Answer: _____ (A.M. or P.M.?)

Use with Lesson 25.

Number Sentences

1. Make up 5 true number sentences and 5 false number sentences. Mix them up. Ask your partner to tell whether each sentence is true or false.

Symbols		
$3 * 4$	$12/3$ $12 \div 3$	$3 < 5$
3×4	$\dfrac{12}{3}$ $3\overline{)12}$	$5 > 3$

a. _____

b. _____

c. _____

d. _____

e. _____

f. _____

g. _____

h. _____

i. _____

j. _____

Tell whether each sentence is true or false. If it is not possible to tell, write "can't tell" on the answer blank.

2. $28 - 16 = 12$ _____

3. $7 + 3 > 1$ _____

4. $6 = 36 \div 6$ _____

5. $27 + 3 = 5 * 6$ _____

6. $80 - \underline{\ ?\ } = 40$ _____

7. $0 = 4 / 4$ _____

8. $3 * 8 < 30$ _____

9. 2×7

Math Boxes

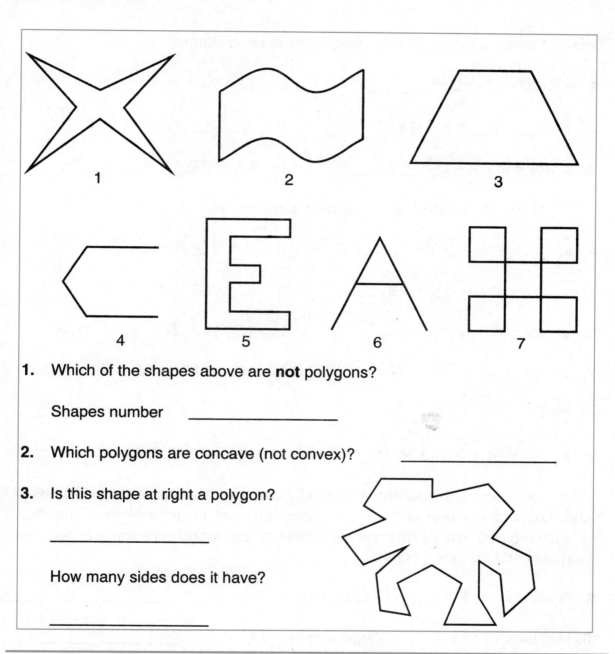

1. Which of the shapes above are **not** polygons?

   Shapes number _____

2. Which polygons are concave (not convex)? _____

3. Is this shape at right a polygon?

   _____

   How many sides does it have?

   _____

☀ Rats

One pair of rats plus its offspring can produce an average of 15,000 young rats in a year; in three years that figure would be over 359 million rats.

It is estimated rats eat an average of about 20% of the world's food crops each year.

Source: Smith, Richard, and Linda Moore. *The Average Book.* New York: The Rutledge Press, 1981.

Use with Lesson 26.

Parentheses in Number Sentences

Part 1: Make a true sentence by filling in the missing number.

1. a. $(30 - 15) * 2 = $ _____   **b.** $30 - (15 * 2) = $ _____

2. a. _____ $= 28 / (14 / 2)$ **b.** _____ $= (28 / 14) / 2$

3. a. $(6 + 8) / (2 - 1) = $ _____   **b.** $6 + (8 / 2) - 1 = $ _____

Part 2: Make a true sentence by inserting parentheses.

4. a. $4 * 9 - 2 = 34$ **b.** $4 * 9 - 2 = 28$

5. a. $24 = 53 - 11 + 18$ **b.** $60 = 53 - 11 + 18$

6. a. $12 / 4 + 2 = 2$ **b.** $12 / 4 + 2 = 5$

7. a. $55 = 15 + 10 \times 4$ **b.** $100 = 15 + 10 \times 4$

Challenge

8. a. $10 - 4 / 2 * 3 = 24$ **b.** $10 - 4 / 2 * 3 = 1$

Part 3: Pretend you are playing a game of *Name That Number* with only 3 cards per hand. Use all 3 numbers and any operations you want to name the target number. For each problem, write a true number sentence, containing parentheses, using the 3 numbers and the target number.

9. Numbers: 2 5 15   Target number: 5   _____

10. Numbers: 3 4 5   Target number: 17   _____

11. Numbers: 1 3 11   Target number: 4   _____

Challenge: Use all 4 numbers to name the target number.

12. Numbers: 4 6 8 10   Target number: 20   _____

Math Boxes

---

1. Solve these problems mentally.

$45,582 - 10 =$ _____

$45,582 + 100 =$ _____

$45,582 + 1000 =$ _____

$45,482 - 10,000 =$ _____

2. Estimate, then measure, the length of your foot, from your heel to your toe.

Estimate:
about _____ _____
                                              unit

Measurement:
about _____ _____
                                              unit

---

3. Write two important things about polygons.

1. _____

_____

2. _____

_____

💡 Keeping Up With the Sun

An amphibious vehicle is a vehicle that can travel both on land and by sea. Imagine that you rode in an amphibious vehicle at sea level along the equator, going west. If you started at noon and traveled at a speed of about 1038 miles per hour, without stopping for a rest, the sun would never set. You would enter a new time zone once an hour, so it would always be noon.

Logic Problems

Math Message

1. There are three children in the Smith family: Sara, Sam, and Sue. Use the following clues to find each one's age.

   - Each of the two younger children is half as old as the next older child.
   - The oldest is 16.
   - Sara is not the oldest.
   - Sara is twice as old as Sam.

   What is the age of each person?

   Sara _____   Sam _____   Sue _____

2. DeeAnn, Eric, Brooke, and Kelsey each has a favorite sport. Each one likes a different sport. Their favorite sports are basketball, swimming, golf, and tennis.

   - DeeAnn doesn't like water.
   - Both Eric and Brooke like to hit a ball.
   - Eric doesn't like to play on a playing field that has lines on it.

   What is each person's favorite sport?

   DeeAnn _____   Eric _____

   Brooke _____   Kelsey _____

3. Raoul, Martha, Kwan, and Karen like to draw. One of them likes working with magic markers best, another with watercolor paints, another with colored chalk, and another with colored pencils.

   - Raoul does not like to work with paint brushes.
   - Martha likes to sharpen her drawing tools.
   - Kwan and Karen do not like dust.
   - Karen sometimes gets bristles in her artwork.

Logic Problems (continued)

Find out what each child likes best. Use the logic grid to help you.

	Magic markers	Watercolor paints	Colored chalk	Colored pencils
Raoul				
Martha				
Kwan				
Karen				

Raoul _____   Martha _____

Kwan _____   Karen _____

4. Sam, Jon, Don, Darla, and Sara each has a favorite kind of cookie. They each like a different kind best.

- Sam and Jon do not like peanut butter.
- Don has never tried sugar cookies and neither has Sara.
- Darla does not like raisins.
- Jon doesn't like sugar cookies.
- Darla and Jon do not like chocolate.
- Sara does like chocolate.
- Don likes fig newtons.

What kind of cookie does each like best? Use the logic grid to help you.

	Peanut butter	Sugar	Fig newtons	Oatmeal raisin	Chocolate fudge
Sam					
Don					
Darla					
Jon					
Sara					

Sam _____   Don _____

Darla _____   Jon _____

Sara _____

Number Sentences and Open Sentences

You may have an older brother or sister who has been taking algebra in school. Have you ever wondered what algebra is all about? Do you think of it as a mysterious subject? If so, it doesn't have to be a mystery anymore, because, in this unit, you have been learning—algebra!

Let's look back at some of the algebra you have been studying. You have learned that **number sentences** are similar to English sentences, except that they use math symbols instead of words. That makes them easier to write down and also easier to work with. So far, you have seen number sentences containing the following math symbols:

- the **digits** 0, 1, 2, 3, 4, 5, 6, 7, 8, 9

- the **operation symbols** +, −, * or ×, and / or ÷

- the symbols <, =, and >; these are called **relation symbols**.

Later on, you will learn about other math symbols.

When a number sentence is made up of these symbols, it is always possible to tell whether it is **true** or **false**. For example, the number sentence 12 + 8 = 20 is true; the number sentence 14 < 10 (14 is less than 10) is false.

There are also sentences in which one of the numbers is missing. We write a letter in place of the missing number. Such sentences are called **open sentences**. The letter that stands for the missing number is called a **variable**. For example, 9 + x = 15 is an open sentence in which the variable x stands for some number. If we replace the letter x with a number, we get a number sentence that is either true or false.

- If we replace x with 10, we get the number sentence 9 + 10 = 15. This sentence is false.

- If we replace x with 6, we get the number sentence 9 + 6 = 15. This sentence is true.

If the number used in place of the variable makes the number sentence true, we call this number the **solution** of the open sentence. For example, the number 6 is the solution of the open sentence 9 + x = 15, because the number sentence 9 + 6 = 15 is true.

And that's all there is to it! The algebra problems will become harder, but the basic ideas you have learned so far will stay the same.

Use with Lesson 30.

Why Do We Need Decimals?

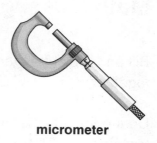

micrometer

You know that we use whole numbers to count things, but that whole numbers may not be useful when we want to make precise measurements. For example, we usually use decimals or fractions to record measurements that are part of a unit, made with a precise instrument, such as a **micrometer**.

A **speedometer** is an instrument that measures how fast a vehicle is traveling. Cars, motorcycles, airplanes, and boats all have a speedometer. You can install a speedometer on any vehicle, even a bicycle. Many common speedometers give only very rough measurements of speed.

Cars also have instruments that measure distance. These are called **odometers**. One kind of odometer displays the total distance the car has traveled since it was driven for the first time. The display usually has 5 digits and shows distance in whole numbers of miles (or in whole numbers of kilometers, outside of the U.S.).

Most cars have a second odometer, called a **trip meter**, which can be set to 0 miles at any time. It is often used to display the distance a car travels from one city to another. For example, if your family went on a vacation by car, you could set the trip meter to 0 at the start of your trip and read the number of miles traveled once you reached your destination.

The car's trip meter is usually a little more precise than the odometer that measures total distance traveled. It measures distance in whole numbers of miles and tenths of miles. The digits that represent whole numbers are usually shown in one color and the digits for tenths of miles in another color.

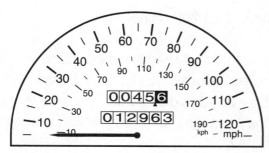

One odometer in the picture shows 12,963. This tells us that the car has traveled at least 12,963 miles so far, but less than 12,964 miles. The trip meter shows 45.6. This means that the car has traveled at least 45.6 miles (45 and 6 tenths) but less than 45.7 miles since the trip meter was set to 0.

Even though decimals look different from whole numbers, you will see that the system we use to record decimals is exactly the same as the system we use to record whole numbers.

Use with Lesson 31.

Math Message: A Bicycle Trip

Bill and Alex often took all-day bicycle trips together.

During the summer, they made a 3-day bicycle tour. They carried camping gear in their saddlebags for the two nights they would be away from home.

Alex had a **trip meter** that showed miles traveled, in tenths of miles. He kept a log of the distances they traveled each day, before and after lunch.

Odometer Readings

	Distance traveled	
	before lunch	after lunch
Day 1	27.0 mi	31.3 mi
Day 2	36.6 mi	20.9 mi
Day 3	25.8 mi	27.0 mi

Use estimation to answer the following questions. Do not work the problems on paper or with a calculator.

1. On which day did they travel the most miles? _____

2. On which day did they travel the fewest miles? _____

3. Did they travel more miles on the whole trip before or after lunch? _____

4. Estimate the total distance they traveled. Circle your estimate.

   a. Less than 150 miles   **b.** Between 150 and 180 miles

   c. Between 180 and 200 miles   **d.** More than 200 miles

5. On Day 1, about how many more miles did they travel after lunch than before lunch?

6. Bill said that they traveled 1.2 more miles before lunch on Day 1 than on Day 3. Alex disagreed. He said that they traveled 2.2 more miles. Who is right?

_____   _____

Forming a Relay Team

Mrs. Wong, the gym teacher, wants to form 3 teams for a 200-yard relay race. There will be 4 students on each team. Each student will run 50 yards.

Mrs. Wong would like the teams to be fairly evenly matched, so she will use the data in the table at the right to help her. The table shows how long it took some fourth-grade students to run 50 yards the last time they had a race. They were timed to the nearest tenth of a second.

She can use these times to try to predict about how long it would take various combinations of students to run the 200-yard relay race.

Here are some combinations she tried. If she uses the times shown in the table, about how long (to the nearest tenth of a second) would the following teams take to run the 200-yard relay race?

50-Yard Race

	Time (seconds)
Art	6.3
Bruce	7.0
John	7.4
Doug	7.9
Al	8.3
Will	8.8
Linda	6.2
Sue	7.6
Pat	7.7
Mary	8.1
Barbara	8.4
Joyce	8.5

1. Art, Bruce, John, Doug   about _____._____ seconds

2. the 4 fastest girls   about _____._____ seconds

3. the 4 slowest students   about _____._____ seconds

4. the 4 fastest students   about _____._____ seconds

5. the 2 fastest and the 2 slowest students   about _____._____ seconds

Challenge

6. Make up 3 teams that will be fairly evenly matched.

Estimated time

Team 1: _____   about _____._____ seconds

Team 2: _____   about _____._____ seconds

Team 3: _____   about _____._____ seconds

7. About how many yards per second did Bruce run?   _____

Use with Lesson 31.

Math Message

Fill in the missing numbers.

1.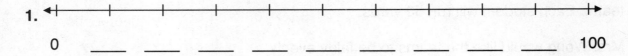

0 ___ ___ ___ ___ ___ ___ ___ ___ ___ 100

2.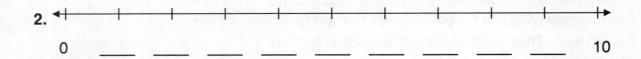

0 ___ ___ ___ ___ ___ ___ ___ ___ ___ 10

3.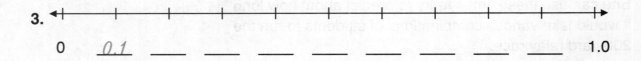

0 *0.1* ___ ___ ___ ___ ___ ___ ___ ___ 1.0

4.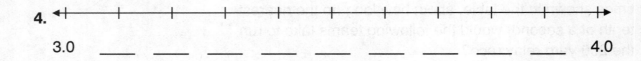

3.0 ___ ___ ___ ___ ___ ___ ___ ___ ___ 4.0

Keeping a Bank Balance

On January 2, Kate's aunt opened a bank account for Kate. She deposited $100.00 into the account.

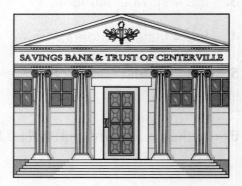

Over the next several months, Kate made regular deposits into her account. She deposited a part of her allowance, and most of the money she made baby-sitting.

Kate also made a few withdrawals—to buy a radio and to buy clothes.

The table on the next page shows the transactions (deposits and withdrawals) Kate made during the first 4 months of the year and the interest earned.

Keeping a Bank Balance (continued)

1. In March, Kate took more money out of her bank account than she put in. In which other month did she withdraw more money than she deposited? _____

2. Complete the table by filling in the current balance for each date. Remember to **add** if Kate makes a deposit or earns interest and to **subtract** if she makes a withdrawal.

Date	Transaction		Current Balance
January 2	Deposit	$100.00	$ _100.00_
January 14	Deposit	$14.23	+ $ _14.23_ $ _114.23_
February 4	Withdraw	$16.50	$ _____ $ _____
February 11	Deposit	$33.75	$ _____ $ _____
February 14	Withdraw	$16.50	$ _____ $ _____
March 19	Deposit	$62.00	$ _____ $ _____
March 30	Withdraw	$104.25	$ _____ $ _____
March 31	Bank credited Kate's account with $0.78 in interest		$ _____ $ _____
April 1	Deposit	$50.60	$ _____ $ _____
April 3	Withdraw	$45.52	$ _____ $ _____
April 9	Withdraw	$27.91	$ _____ $ _____
April 28	Deposit	$18.22	$ _____ $ _____

Check your answers with a partner.

Use with Lesson 32.

Math Boxes

---

1. Choose a fact triangle. Write the fact family for it.

  a. _____ * _____ = _____

  b. _____ * _____ = _____

  c. _____ / _____ = _____

  d. _____ / _____ = _____

2. In each of the following, write a number that makes the sentence true.

  a. 5 * _____ > 20

  b. 5 * _____ < 20

  c. 8 * _____ < 80

  d. 9 * _____ > 99

---

3. Write 4,007,392 using words.

  _____

  _____

  _____

  _____

4. Make true sentences by inserting parentheses.

  a. 5 * 4 − 2 = 18

  b. 25 + 8 * 7 = 81

  c. 36 / 6 − 5 = 1

  d. 81 / 9 + 15 = 24

---

5. List the names of the countries on page 32 in your *World Tour Book* whose flags have a triangle.

  _____

  _____

  _____

  _____

Use with Lesson 32.

Will I Run Out of Gas?

You are driving with your family from Denver, Colorado to Des Moines, Iowa. You know the following:

- Your car's gasoline tank holds about 12.1 gallons.
- Your car uses about 1 gallon of gasoline for every 30 miles on the highway.
- You start your trip with a full tank.

Here is a map of the route you follow.

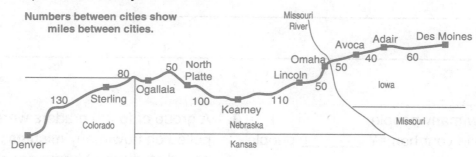

Numbers between cities show miles between cities.

1. About how many gallons of gasoline would your car use from Denver to Sterling?   about _____ gallons

2. When you get to Ogallala, would you expect your gas tank to be:

   a. almost empty   **b.** about $\frac{1}{4}$ full   **c.** about $\frac{1}{2}$ full   **d.** about $\frac{3}{4}$ full

3. Is it O.K. to wait until you get to Kearney to buy more gas? _____
   Explain.

   _____

   _____

   _____

4. You decide to stop at North Platte to buy more gasoline. If you buy 7.6 gallons, about how many gallons are there in your tank now?   _____

5. Could you get to Des Moines from North Platte without running out of gas, if you filled your gasoline tank just one more time?   _____

   If so, where would you stop?   _____

Use with Lesson 33.

Math Boxes

1. Write 4 names for 100.

    a. _____

    b. _____

    c. _____

    d. _____

2. How many people
live in your home? _____ people

How many of the people
who live in your home
are female? _____ females

What fraction of the people
who live in your home
are female?

_____ are female.

3. A group of fourth graders were
polled on how many minutes they
spend studying at home per week.
Here are the responses from 10
students:

    130, 45, 240, 35, 160,
    185, 120, 20, 55, 160

What is the mode? _____

What is the median? _____

 ## Wasted Fuel

In one day, Americans lose one million gallons of gasoline to evaporation at gas
stations and other gasoline fueling facilities. That is enough to fuel the average car
for 2,000 years.

Source: Parker, Tom. *In One Day*. Boston: Houghton Mifflin, 1984.

Use with Lesson 33.

Measuring Air Pressure with a Barometer

Some people think that air doesn't weigh anything. But it does—you can prove this to yourself by doing a simple experiment: Weigh a deflated soccer ball or basketball and then pump it full of air. The ball will weigh more after you have pumped air into it. This shows that the air you pumped in does have weight.

In 1643, Torricelli, a student of Galileo, invented an instrument for measuring **air pressure**—how much the weight of air pushes down on a surface. He made a glass tube about $3\frac{1}{2}$ feet long, closed it at one end, and filled it with mercury. Then he turned the tube upside down and put it into an open jar containing more mercury. When he did that, the mercury in the tube fell a few inches and then stopped.

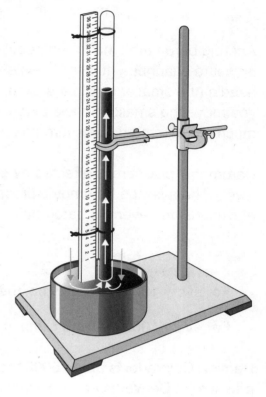

You may wonder why some of the mercury remained in the tube. Why did it not all flow out of the tube and mix with the mercury in the jar? The reason is that the air above the jar pushes down on the mercury in the jar. This, in turn, supports the mercury in the tube. The greater the air pressure, the higher the level of the mercury in the tube.

The instrument Torricelli invented is called a **mercury barometer**. The height of the mercury in the tube depends on the **barometric pressure**. When a weather forecaster reports that the barometric pressure is 30.25, this means that the mercury in the tube has reached a level of 30.25 inches.

Barometers are used to predict the weather. In fact, Torricelli's barometer came to be known as the "weather glass." When the weather pattern is changing, the barometric pressure changes. When the barometer readings fall steadily or suddenly, a storm is probably on its way. The faster the barometer readings fall and the lower the reading, the more severe the storm is likely to be. When the barometer readings rise, you may expect fair weather.

Use with Lesson 34.

aneroid barometer

Mercury barometers are awkward to carry from one place to another. A more convenient type of barometer is the **aneroid barometer**. This is the sort of barometer you may have in your school or at home. Aneroid means "without liquid." The units on an aneroid barometer have the same meaning as the units on a mercury barometer. If your aneroid barometer reads 29.85, a mercury barometer would show 29.85 inches of mercury in the tube.

Aneroid barometers have two needles. One needle moves, when the barometric pressure changes. (It is the needle that points to 30 in the picture.) The other needle (the smaller one in the picture) stays in place unless someone moves it. If you move the smaller needle to today's reading, you will be able to measure how much the barometric pressure has changed later on.

Barometric pressure is affected by **elevation**—how high the barometer is above sea level. The average barometric pressure at sea level is about 30 inches. At higher elevations, the average barometric pressure will be less. Can you explain why?

The Elevation Rule:

• For every 100 feet you climb, the barometer reading will drop about 0.1 inch.

• For every 1000 feet you climb, it will drop about 1 inch.

Denver, Colorado, is about 5000 feet above sea level; the average barometric pressure in Denver is about 25 inches.

Here is a map of the island of Hawaii. The numbers on the map give barometer readings for the cities shown, at the same time, under similar weather conditions. All readings were taken at the same time. They vary because cities have different heights above sea level.

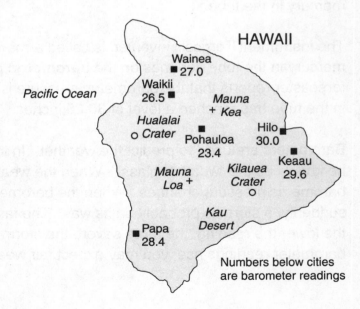

HAWAII

Pacific Ocean

Wainea ■ 27.0

Waikii 26.5 ■

Hualalai ○ Crater

Mauna + Kea

Pohauloa 23.4

Hilo 30.0 ■

Mauna Loa +

Kilauea Crater ○

Keaau 29.6 ■

Kau Desert

Papa ■ 28.4

Numbers below cities are barometer readings

The Barometer and Elevation

Refer to the map of Hawaii and the Elevation Rule on page 76.

1. Hilo is the largest city on the island of Hawaii. It
    is at sea level. This means that its elevation is
    0 feet above sea level. What is the barometer
    reading in Hilo?   about _____ inches

2. **a.** What is the barometer reading in Keaau?   about _____ inches

    b. What is the barometer reading in Wainea?   about _____ inches

    c. Which is higher above sea level—
        Keaau or Wainea?   _____

3. **a.** What is the barometer reading in Waikii?   about _____ inches

    b. How much less is the barometer reading
        in Waikii than in Hilo?   _____ inches less

    c. What is the elevation of Waikii?   about _____ feet above sea level

4. The barometer reading at the top of Kilauea Crater is
    1.7 inches less than at the top of Hualalai Crater.

    a. Which crater has a higher elevation?   _____

    b. About how much higher is it?   about _____ feet

5. The Kau Desert is about 2500 feet above sea
    level. What should the barometer reading be
    there?   about _____ inches

6. The highest mountains on Hawaii are Mauna Loa and
    Mauna Kea. Their heights are nearly the same. If the
    barometer reads 16.4 inches at the top of these mountains,
    what is their elevation?

                                        about _____ feet above sea level

Use with Lesson 34.

Math Boxes

---

1. Five students each had six coins. How many coins were there all together?

_____ coins

Number model:

_____

2. I am a whole number. Use the clues to figure out what number I am.

Clue 1: I am less than 100.
Clue 2: The sum of my digits is 4.
Clue 3: Half of me is an odd number.

What number am I? _____

---

3. What time is it? Answer to the nearest minute.

_____ : _____ P.M.

4. Use the clock in Box 3 to answer the following questions.
What time was it 35 minutes ago?

_____ : _____ P.M.

What time will it be in 25 minutes?

_____ : _____ P.M.

It will be 4:30 P.M. in _____ minutes.

---

5. There are 72 X's in an array with 8 equal rows. Draw the array.

How many X's are
in each row?   _____

Decimals and Metric Units

Symbols for Metric Units of Length	
meter	m
decimeter	dm
centimeter	cm
millimeter	mm

1 m = 10 dm   1 dm = 0.1 m

	1 dm
0	

1 decimeter

1 m = 100 cm   1 cm = 0.01 m
1 dm = 10 cm   1 cm = 0.1 dm

0 1 2 3 4 5 6 7 8 9 10 cm

10 centimeters

1 m = 1000 mm   1 mm = 0.001 m
1 dm = 100 mm   1 mm = 0.01 dm
1 cm = 10 mm   1 mm = 0.1 cm

0 10 20 30 40 50 60 70 80 90 100 mm

100 millimeters

Use your tape measure to help you fill in the answers.

Challenge

1. a.   5 cm = _____ mm   b.   4.2 cm = _____ mm   c.   0.8 cm = _____ mm

2. a.   30 mm = _____ cm   b.   64 mm = _____ cm   c.   5 mm = _____ cm

3. a.   3 m = _____ cm   b.   2.6 m = _____ cm   c.   0.43 m = _____ cm

4. a.   500 cm = _____ m   b.   780 cm = _____ m   c.   65 cm = _____ m

5. a.   4 m = _____ mm   b.   6.1 m = _____ mm   c.   0.750 m = _____ mm

6.   Draw a line segment about 12.5 centimeters long. Use a sharp pencil.

Math Boxes

1. A number has

5 thousands
2 hundred thousands
3 ones
0 hundreds
6 millions
0 tens
4 ten thousands

Write the number. _____

2. Make the smallest possible whole number using the digits from Box 1.

5 2 3 0 6 0 4

A zero can not be the first digit.

__ __ __ __ __ __ __

3. Make the largest possible whole number using the digits from Box 1.

5 2 3 0 6 0 4

__ __ __ __ __ __ __

4. Use your calculator to add your answers from Box 2 and Box 3 together.

Answer: _____

5. Draw a quadrangle with 2 pairs of parallel sides.

What kind of quadrangle is this?

_____

Use with Lesson 36.

Math Message

Fill in the missing numbers.

1.
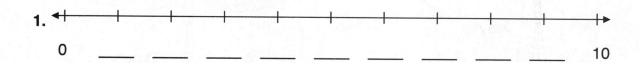

0   10

2.
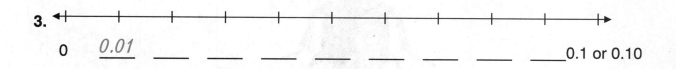

0   *0.1*   1 or 1.0

3.
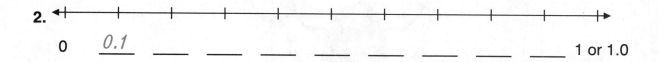

0   *0.01*   0.1 or 0.10

4.
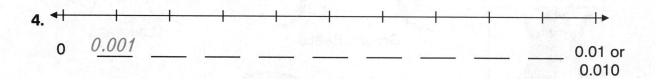

0   *0.001*   0.01 or
                                                                                   0.010

Measuring Land Invertebrates

An **invertebrate** is an animal that does not have a backbone. (The backbone is also called the **spinal column**.) Some invertebrates live on land, others in the water. The most common land invertebrates are insects.

All the invertebrates shown on page 82, except the bee and the mealybug, have been drawn to about actual size. The bee is drawn to about twice its actual size and the mealybug to about 3 times its actual size.

All the animals, except the earthworm, can grow to be about as large as in the pictures. However, earthworms can grow to about 4 times the length shown here.

Use with Lesson 37.

Land Invertebrates

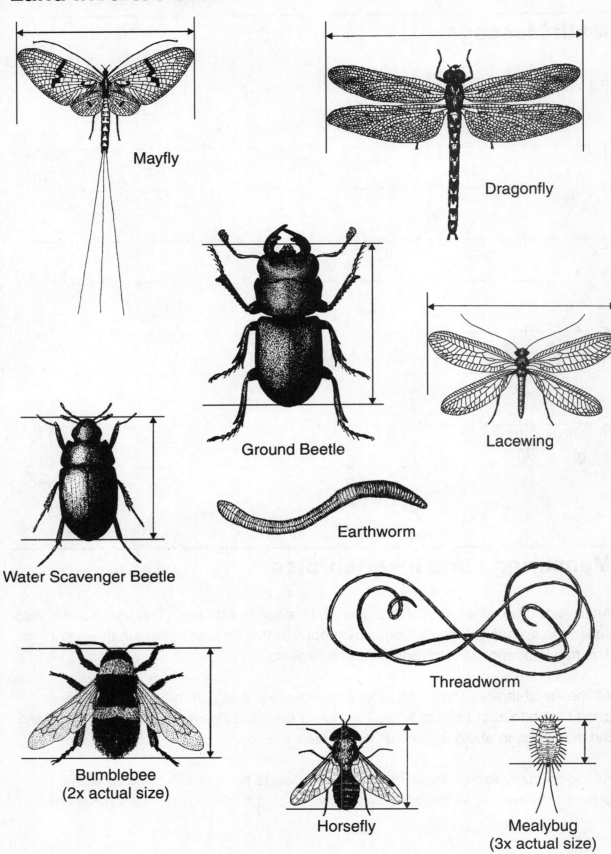

Mayfly

Dragonfly

Ground Beetle

Lacewing

Water Scavenger Beetle

Earthworm

Threadworm

Bumblebee
(2x actual size)

Horsefly

Mealybug
(3x actual size)

Measuring Land Invertebrates (continued)

1 meter (m) = 10 decimeters (dm)	1 dm = 0.1 m
1 m = 100 centimeters (cm)	1 cm = 0.01 m
1 m = 1000 millimeter (mm)	1 mm = 0.001 m

1. Refer to the pictures on page 82. Measure the following invertebrates to the nearest millimeter by finding the distance between the two guidelines.

   a. mayfly: about _____ mm   **b.** dragonfly: about _____ mm

   c. water beetle: about _____ mm   **d.** ground beetle: about _____ mm

   e. lacewing: about _____ mm   **f.** horsefly: about _____ mm

2. Give the length of the ground beetle and water beetle in centimeters.

   ground beetle: about _____ cm   water beetle: about _____ cm

   How much longer is the ground beetle than
   the water beetle?   about _____ cm

3. The bee has been drawn to twice its actual size.
   Which is longer, the bee or the horsefly?   _____

   How much longer?   about _____ mm

4. When straight, the earthworm in the drawing is about
   8 centimeters long. What is its length in meters?   about _____ m

5. When straight, the threadworm in the drawing is about
   306 millimeters long.

   What is its length in centimeters?   about _____ cm

   In meters?   about _____ m

6. Which is longer, the earthworm or the threadworm?   _____

7. The mealybug has been drawn to 3 times
   its actual size. Draw a mealybug that is
   about the right size.

Use with Lesson 37.

Math Boxes

1. The shortest adult in the world was $22\frac{1}{2}$ inches tall. This is between:
 	
  a. 0 and 1 foot
 	
  b. 1 and 2 feet
 	
  c. 2 and 3 feet
 	
  d. 3 and 4 feet
 	
Write the letter for the correct answer: _____
	2. 5 children share 27 tennis balls equally.
	
	Each child gets _____ balls.
	
	There are _____ balls left over.

3. I am a whole number. Use the clues to figure out what number I am. Clue 1: If you multiply me by 2, I become a number greater than 20 and less than 40. Clue 2: If you multiply me by 6, I end in 8. Clue 3: I am an odd number. What number am I? _____	**4.** Draw a shape that has no parallel sides.

 ## Fish

The 9-inch archer fish can shoot a stream of water an average of 3 to 4 feet to knock its insect food out of the air.

The average lifespan of a goldfish is about 14 years.

A bluefin tuna's swimming speed averages 60 miles per hour.

African Rhinos

Read pages 6 and 7 in your *World Tour Book*. Then answer the following questions.

1. About how many rhinos are there left in all of Africa?   about _____ rhinos

2. South Africa has taken steps to protect its rhino
   population. What kind of rhinos live there?   _____

3. A poacher wants to sell the horns of a black rhino.

   a. About how many pounds do both horns weigh?   about _____ pounds

   b. At $1500 a pound, about how much would he get
      for the horns?   about $ _____

   c. A typical worker in Zaire earns about $1 per day.
      About how many days would this worker have to
      work to earn enough money to buy the rhino's
      horns?   about _____ days

   d. About how many years would he have to work?   about _____ years

4. About 6600 pounds of illegal rhino horns were traded
   each year during the 1980s. About how many rhinos
   were killed each year?   about _____ rhinos

5. About how many rhinos were killed during the 10-year
   period from 1980 to 1990?   about _____ rhinos

Compare the number of rhinos killed from 1980 to 1990 with the number of rhinos
that remain today. Unless something is done to protect the rhinos, there soon won't
be any left.

Rules for *Getting to One* Game

Materials: calculator

Number of players: 2

Object of the game:

One player chooses a mystery number. The other player tries to guess the number in as few tries as possible. Players then trade roles. The player who guessed the mystery number in fewer tries wins the round.

Directions:

1. Player A chooses a mystery number less than 100.
2. Player A then secretly enters the number in the calculator and divides it by itself. For example, if the mystery number is 65, Player A enters 65 [÷] 65 [=]. (On calculators with a [K] key, enter 65 [÷] 65 [K] [=].) The result should be 1.
3. Player B guesses the mystery number and, without clearing the calculator, enters the guess and [=] in the calculator.
   - If the calculator shows a number less than 1, then the guess was too low.
   - If it shows a number greater than 1, then the guess was too large.
   - If it shows a 1, then Player B guessed the mystery number.

Player B enters guesses until the result is 1. Player A keeps track of the number of guesses. **Do not clear the calculator until the number has been guessed.**

Example: Mystery number = 65

Player B enters:	Calculator shows:	
55 [=]	0.8461538	too small
70 [=]	1.076923	too big
67 [=]	1.0307692	too big, but closer
65 [=]	1	Just right!

It took Player B four tries to guess the mystery number.

Scoring:

One way is to play 5 rounds in which there were no ties. The player who won more rounds wins the game.

Another way is to play 5 rounds and to keep track of the number of guesses for each round. The player with fewer guesses in all wins the game.

For a harder version of the game, allow mystery numbers up to 1000.

Use with Lesson 39.

Math Boxes

1. 85 fourth graders want to attend a field trip next Saturday at the local museum. The children must ride in vans that hold 7 passengers. How many vans are needed so that all the students get to go on the field trip? Show how you solved the problem.

   _____

2. Make up a number story for 2906 − 568 = _____ . Then solve the problem and share your strategy for solving the problem.

   _____

   _____

   _____

   _____

   _____

3. Ray, Samantha, Josh, and Erica each have a different after-school snack as their favorite: ice cream, pretzels, potato chips, or cookies. Find out which snack is the favorite for each child. (Hint: Use a logic grid if you need help.)

   • Josh does not like salty snacks.
   • Ray likes a snack that is cold and comes in a lot of different flavors.
   • Samantha likes a snack that is salty and may sometimes be twisted.

   Ray _____   Samantha _____

   Josh _____   Erica _____

Our System for Recording Numbers

Our system for recording numbers is a **base-ten** system. This should come as no surprise to you—most people have 10 fingers and when people first started using numbers, they probably counted on their fingers.

In the beginning, the system for writing numbers was very primitive. Perhaps, people used a special symbol to show a count of 10 and another symbol to show a count of 1. We know that the ancient Egyptians used a stroke to record the number 1, a picture of an oxen yoke for 10, a coil of rope for 100, and a lotus plant for 1000. For 1,000,000, they used a picture of a god supporting the sky.

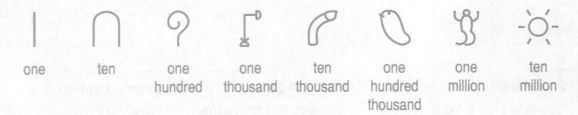

| one | ten | one hundred | one thousand | ten thousand | one hundred thousand | one million | ten million |

This is how they would write the number 43:

$$10 + 10 + 10 + 10 + 1 + 1 + 1$$

Our base-ten system was invented in India and later improved in Arabia. It uses just ten symbols, called **digits**: 0, 1, 2, 3, 4, 5, 6, 7, 8, and 9. In this system, you can write any number you wish using some or all of the 10 digits.

In a number written in the base-ten system, each digit has a value that depends on its **place** in the number. This is why our base-ten system is

1000's	100's	10's	1's
Thousands	Hundreds	Tens	Ones
6	0	7	5

called a **place-value** system. For example, in the number 6075, the digit 6 is in the **thousands** place; its value is 6000. The digit 0 is in the **hundreds** place; the value of 0 hundreds is 0. The 7 is in the **tens** place; its value is 70. The 5 is in the **ones** place; its value is 5.

What would happen if our base-ten system did not have the digit 0? For example, how would you use digits to write six thousand seventy-five? The 0 in 6075 serves a very important purpose: It "holds" the hundreds place so that the 6 can be in the thousands place. When used in this way, 0 is called a **placeholder**.

Notice what happens as you move from right to left in the place-value chart:
The value of each place increases tenfold.

- The value of the tens place is 10 times the value of the ones place ($10 \times 1 = 10$).

- The value of the hundreds place is 10 times the value of the tens place ($10 \times 10 = 100$).

- The value of the thousands place is 10 times the value of the hundreds place ($10 \times 100 = 1000$).

What happens when you move the other way, from left to right? The value of each place is **one-tenth** of the value of the place to its left.

- The value of the hundreds place is one-tenth of the value of the thousands place ($\frac{1}{10}$ of 1000 = 100).

- The value of the tens place is one-tenth of the value of the hundreds place ($\frac{1}{10}$ of 100 = 10).

- The value of the ones place is one-tenth of the value of the tens place ($\frac{1}{10}$ of 10 = 1).

Let's keep on going.

- The value of the place to the right of the ones place is one-tenth of the value of the ones place: One-tenth of 1 is one-tenth. We call this place the **tenths** place.

- The value of the place to the right of the tenths place is one-tenth of the value of the tenths place: One-tenth of one-tenth is one-hundredth, or 0.01. We call this place the **hundredths** place.

- The value of the place to the right of the hundredths place is one-tenth of the value of the hundredths place: One-tenth of one-hundredth is one-thousandth, or 0.001. We call this place the **thousandths** place.

1000's	100's	10's	1's		0.1's	0.01's	0.001's
Thousands	Hundreds	Tens	Ones	.	Tenths	Hundredths	Thousandths
		3	6	.	7	0	4

The base-ten system works the same way for decimal numbers as it does for whole numbers. For example, in the number 36.704, the digit 7 is in the **tenths** place; its value is 7 tenths. The digit 0 is in the **hundredths** place; the value of 0 hundredths is 0. The 4 is in the **thousandths** place; its value is 4 thousandths. The number 36.704 can be read as 36 and 704 thousandths.

Use with Lesson 40.

Multiplying Ones and Tens

You can extend a multiplication fact by making tens of one of the factors.

> **Example:**
>
> Original fact: 2 * 3 = 6
>
> Extended facts: 2 * 30 = _____ or 20 * 3 = _____
>
> Write the products.

Copy multiplication facts from 4 Fact Triangles. Then extend each fact by writing one of the factors in the original fact as tens.

1. Original fact   _____

   Extended fact   _____

2. Original fact   _____

   Extended fact   _____

3. Original fact   _____

   Extended fact   _____

4. Original fact   _____

   Extended fact   _____

What shortcut can you use to multiply ones and tens, for example, 3 * 60?

_____

_____

_____

_____

Multiplying Tens

You can extend a multiplication fact by making tens of both factors.

Example:

Original fact: 5 * 9 = 45

Extended fact: **50 * 90** = _____

Write the product.

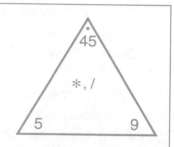

Copy multiplication facts from 4 Fact Triangles. Then extend each fact by writing both factors in the original fact as tens.

1. Original fact _____

Extended fact _____

2. Original fact _____

Extended fact _____

3. Original fact _____

Extended fact _____

4. Original fact _____

Extended fact _____

What shortcut can you use to multiply tens, for example, 50 * 90?

_____

_____

_____

_____

Use with Lesson 41.

Date _____ Time _____

Beat the Calculator

Materials: 1 deck of number cards 1–10 (4 of each for a total of 40 cards)
calculator

Number of players: 3

Directions: One player is the
"caller," a second player is the
"calculator," and the third player is
the "brain."

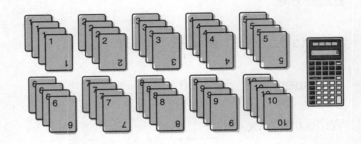

Shuffle the deck of cards and place it face down on the playing surface.
The caller—

• Turns over the top two cards from the deck;

• Attaches a 0 to either one of the factors or to both factors.

For example, if the "caller" turns over a 4 and a 6, he or she may make up one of the
following problems:

$$4 * 60 \qquad 40 * 6 \qquad 40 * 60$$

The "calculator" finds the product with a calculator, while the "brain" solves it without
a calculator. The "caller" decides who got the answer first.

Players trade roles every 10 turns or so.

Animal Facts

A polar bear can smell a human as much as 20 miles away.

An elephant eats an average of 500 pounds of food a day.

An electric eel can kill a person at a distance of about 15 feet by discharging an
electric shock.

Source: Smith, Richard, and Linda Moore. *The Average Book*. New York: The Rutledge Press, 1981.

Use with Lesson 41.

Multiplication Wrestling (2-Digit Numbers)

Materials: a deck of 0–9 number cards
(4 of each number for a total of 40 cards)

Number of players: 2

Object: To get the largest product of two
2-digit numbers.

Directions: Shuffle the deck of cards and place it face down. Each player draws
4 cards and forms two 2-digit numbers. There are many possible combinations of
2-digit numbers. Each player must pick a pair of numbers to use.

Example:

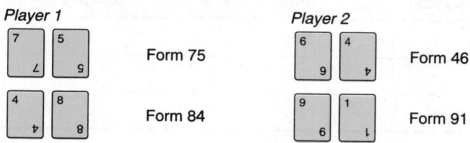

Player 1

| 7 | 5 |

Form 75

| 4 | 8 |

Form 84

Player 2

| 6 | 4 |

Form 46

| 9 | 1 |

Form 91

Each player creates two "wrestling teams" by writing each number as a sum of tens
and ones.

	Player 1:		Player 2:
	75 * 84		46 * 91
Teams:	(70 + 5) * (80 + 4)		(40 + 6) * (90 + 1)

Next, each player's two wrestling teams wrestle each other in this way:
Each member of the first team (for example, 70 and 5) is multiplied by
each member of the second team (for example, 80 and 4). Then the four
products are added.

Player 1:

$$(70 + 5) \quad * \quad (80 + 4)$$

$$(70 * 80) + (70 * 4) + (5 * 80) + (5 * 4) =$$

$$5600 + 280 + 400 + 20 = 6300$$

```
  5 6 0 0
    2 8 0
    4 0 0
+    2 0
  5 0 0 0
  1 2 0 0
    1 0 0
  6 3 0 0
```

Use with Lesson 42.

Player 2:

$$(40 + 6) \;*\; (90 + 1)$$

$$(40 * 90) + (40 * 1) + (6 * 90) + (6 * 1) =$$

$$3600 \;+\; 40 \;+\; 540 \;+\; 6 \;=\; 4186$$

```
  3 6 0 0
      4 0
    5 4 0
+       6
  3 0 0 0
  1 1 0 0
      8 0
        6
  4 1 8 6
```

The player with the larger result wins the round. To find the winner's score, subtract the loser's result from the winner's result and record the difference on a score sheet like the one below. For example, Player 1 scores 2114 points because 6300 − 4186 = 2114. Player 2 scores no points.

Players' Names:	Player 1	Player 2
Round 1	2114	0
Round 2		
Round 3		
Total		

In each round, each player forms two new numbers. Decide ahead of time on how many rounds or how long to play. At the end of the game, players add their scores. The player with the largest total wins.

Players may use a calculator to find the winner's score for a round and their total score for the game. They may also use a calculator to check a player's score for a round by multiplying the two numbers. (For example, to check Player 1's score, multiply 75 * 84.)

☀ Survival Rule of Three

You can live three seconds without blood, three minutes without air, three days without water, and three weeks without food.

Source: Parker, Tom. *Rules of Thumb.* Boston: Houghton Mifflin, 1983.

Use with Lesson 42.

Date _____ Time _____

Multiplication Wrestling Score Sheet

Players' Names:		
Round 1		
Round 2		
Round 3		
Round 4		
Round 5		
Round 6		
Round 7		
Round 8		
Total		

Players' Names:		
Round 1		
Round 2		
Round 3		
Round 4		
Round 5		
Round 6		
Round 7		
Round 8		
Total		

Use with Lesson 42.

Math Boxes

1. Solve the following open sentences using your calculator. The [−] key is broken, however. Record your key strokes.

   a. $43 + x = 518$ Key strokes: _____

   Solution: _____

   b. $q + 683 = 1274$ Key strokes: _____

   Solution: _____

2. $3 + 4 = 7$

   $7 = 4 + 3$

   Both of the number sentences above are true. What about the ones below? Tell if they are true or false.

   $12 \div 4 = 3$ _____

   $3 = 4 \div 12$ _____

3. The after-school pep rally was over at 3:45 P.M. It lasted for 30 minutes. At what time did the rally start?

   _____

☀ Under Water

If the earth was level, all of its water would cover it with a layer 1.5 miles deep.

If all the ice above sea level were to melt, the sea would rise 130 feet. Flat coastal regions, such as Florida, and a good many islands would disappear.

Source: Houwink, R. *Did You Know?* Mahwah, New Jersey: Watermill Press, 1989.

A Map of the North Section of Alaska

Allakaket	D-3
Ambler	C-3
Anaktuvuk Pass	D-4
Arctic Village	E-4
Barrow	D-5
Birch Creek	E-3
Circle	F-2
Delta Junction	F-2
Evansville	D-3
Holy Cross	C-1
Hooper Bay	A-1
Kaktovik	F-4
Kivalina	B-4
Kotzebue	B-3
McGrath	C-1
Nenana	E-2
Nikolai	D-1
Nome	B-2
Noorvik	C-3
Point Hope	B-4
Ruby	D-2
Russian Mission	B-1
Stebbins	B-2
Usibelli Mine	E-2
Wainwright	C-5
Wales	A-3

A Campground Map

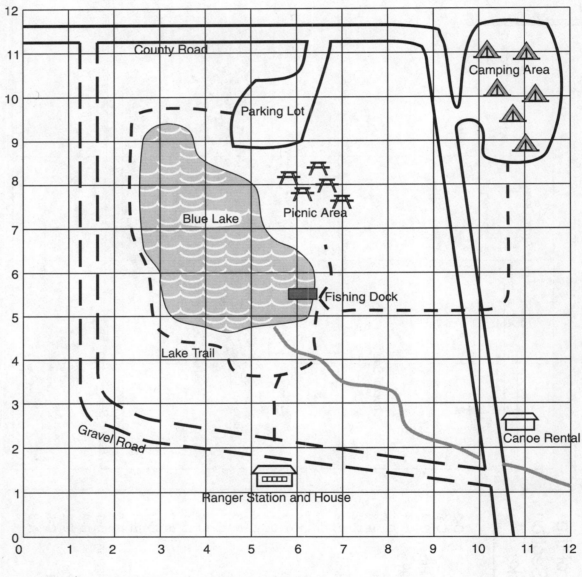

SCALE

| 0 | 0.2 | 0.4 | 0.6 | 0.8 | 1 km |

County Road

Parking Lot

Camping Area

Blue Lake

Picnic Area

Fishing Dock

Lake Trail

Gravel Road

Canoe Rental

Ranger Station and House

Legend:

———————	Paved Road	
– – – – –	Unpaved Road	
- - - - -	Trail	
———————	River	

Camping Area

Picnic Area

Finding Distances on a Map

Use the campground map on page 98 to complete the following.

1. Suppose you hiked along the Lake Trail from the
   Fishing Dock to the Parking Lot. Estimate the
   distance you hiked.   about _____ km

2. The ranger is making her hourly round. She starts at
   the Ranger Station, drives northwest and then north
   to the County Road, then on the County Road past
   the Parking Lot, the Camping Area, and the Canoe
   Rental, back to the Ranger Station. About what
   distance did she drive?   about _____ km

3. Estimate the distance around Blue Lake.   about _____ km

4. You are planning to hike from the camping area to the parking lot. You want to
   hike a distance of at least 5 kilometers, always staying on the roads or trails.

   a. Plan your route. Then draw it on the map with a colored pencil or crayon.

   b. Estimate the distance.   about _____ km

5. Label the location of each of the following on the map.

	Location	Label
parked car	(5,9)	C
boat	$(3\frac{1}{2},8)$	B
swing set	(8,11)	S
hikers	(10.5,6.5)	H
farmhouse	$(\frac{1}{2},7)$	F

Use with Lesson 43.

Math Boxes

1. Complete the multiplication and division facts.

$9 * \underline{\hspace{1.5cm}} = 27$

$5 * \underline{\hspace{1.5cm}} = 35$

$45 / 9 = \underline{\hspace{1.5cm}}$

$64 / \underline{\hspace{1.5cm}} = 8$

$72 / 8 = \underline{\hspace{1.5cm}}$

$8 * 6 = \underline{\hspace{1.5cm}}$

2. Name the shaded area as a decimal.

_____

3. Shade 0.29 of the grid at right. How much more would you need to shade to get 0.70?

_____

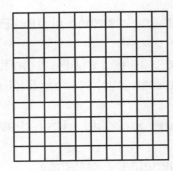

4. Tell if each of these is closer to a millimeter, centimeter, 10 centimeters, or a meter.

a. width of your finger _____

b. thickness of your fingernail _____

c. width of your shoe _____

d. length of your leg _____

Use with Lesson 43.

Making an Angle Measurer

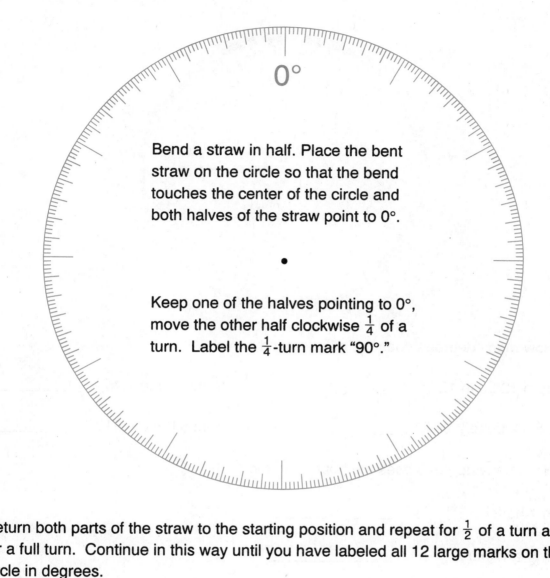

0°

Bend a straw in half. Place the bent straw on the circle so that the bend touches the center of the circle and both halves of the straw point to 0°.

Keep one of the halves pointing to 0°, move the other half clockwise $\frac{1}{4}$ of a turn. Label the $\frac{1}{4}$-turn mark "90°."

Return both parts of the straw to the starting position and repeat for $\frac{1}{2}$ of a turn and for a full turn. Continue in this way until you have labeled all 12 large marks on the circle in degrees.

The Babylonians lived about 2500 years ago in the part of the world that includes the central region of present-day Iraq. Babylon was on the Euphrates River, not far from Baghdad, the current capital of Iraq.

The Babylonians used a numbering system based on the number 60. (As you know, our numbering system is based on the number 10.) We do use Babylonian ideas in the way we measure time: We divide the hour into 60 minutes and the minute into 60 seconds. We also use the number 60 in measuring angles: A full turn measures 360° and 360 is a multiple of 60 (6 × 60 = 360).

Clock Angles

1. How many degrees does the minute hand move:

    from 12:00 to 12:30? _____   from 1:00 to 1:15? _____

    from 2:00 to 2:05? _____   from 5:00 to 5:01? _____

2. How many degrees does the hour hand move

    in 1 hour?   _____

    in $\frac{1}{2}$ an hour?   _____

    in 10 minutes?   _____

Brain teasers

★ 3. How long does it take the hour hand to move 1°?   _____
       (**Hint:** How many degrees does it move in 10 minutes?)

★ 4. How long does it take the minute hand to move 1°?   _____
       (**Hint:** How many degrees does it move in 1 minute?)

Use with Lesson 45.

Measuring Angles with a 360° Angle Measurer

Use your angle measurer to measure each angle.

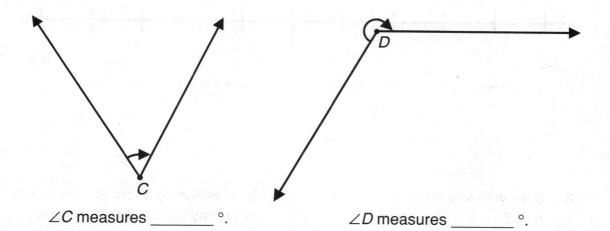

∠C measures _____°.   ∠D measures _____°.

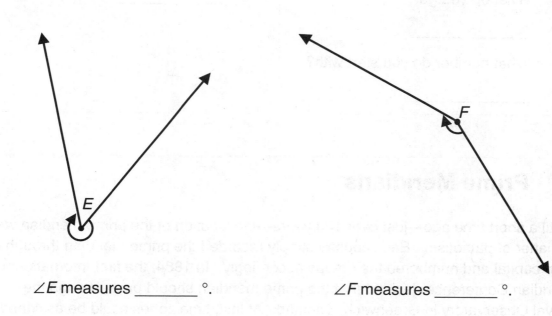

∠E measures _____°.   ∠F measures _____°.

Date _____ Time _____

Math Boxes

1. Fill in the missing values. You may use your calculator to help you.

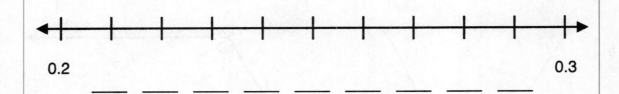

0.2   0.3

---

2. Start with any number.
Add 5.
Double the result.
Subtract 10.
Take half.
What do you get?

_____

What number do you start with?

_____

3. It takes Sandy about 50 minutes to get ready for school. If the bus comes by at 7:50 A.M., about what time should she get up?

_____

 ## Prime Meridians

Until a short time ago—just over 100 years—the location of the prime meridian was a matter of patriotism. Each country simply recorded the prime meridian through its own capital and numbered their maps accordingly. In 1884, the first International Meridian Conference decided that the prime meridian should pass through the Royal Observatory in Greenwich, England. At last, time zones could be assigned to the world.

Source: Blocksma, Mary. *Reading the Numbers.* New York: Viking Penguin Inc., 1989.

Math Message

Use a straightedge to draw the following angles. Do not use an angle measurer.

∠A: any angle
less than 90°

∠B: any angle more than
90° and less than 180°

∠C: any angle
more than 180°

∠A is called an
acute angle.

∠B is called an
obtuse angle.

∠C is called a
reflex angle.

Measuring Angles with a Protractor

Measure each angle as accurately as you can.

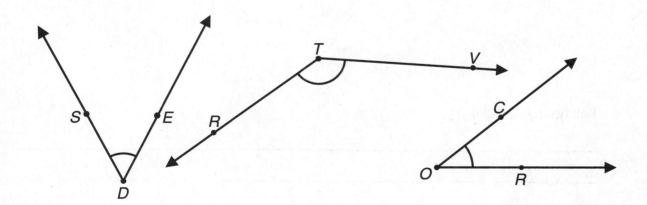

∠SDE is about _____°.　　∠RTV is about _____°.　　∠COR is about _____°.

Date ______________________ Time ______________

Drawing Angles with a Protractor

1. Draw and label the following angles. Use a protractor.

$\angle DTG$: 72°

$\angle SOW$: 125°

Challenge

2. Use a protractor to draw a 250° angle. Label it with 3 letters.

Tell how you did it.

____

____

____

____

____

Use with Lesson 47.

Angle Drawing Practice

1. Draw a 15° angle, using
   ray *AB* as one of its sides.

2. Draw a 150° angle, using
   ray *CD* as one of its sides.

3. Draw a 60° angle, using
   ray *EF* as one of its sides.

4. Draw a 48° angle, using
   segment *GH* as one of its sides.

5. Draw a 125° angle, using
   ray *IJ* as one of its sides.

Math Boxes

1. Name an item in your classroom that measures about:

   1 millimeter   _____

   1 centimeter   _____

   1 meter   _____

   Try to use items that you have not already measured in previous lessons.

2. Make up a set of 5 numbers having the following landmarks:

   median = 8
   range = 10
   minimum = 3

   _____ , _____, _____, _____, _____

3. Shade 0.89 of the grid at right.
   How much more would you
   need to shade to get 1.0?

   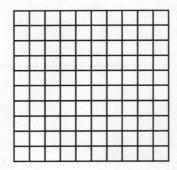

   _____

Latitude and Longitude

Use the world map and globe in your classroom to answer the questions.

1. Find the longitude and latitude of each of these locations.

Location	Longitude	Latitude
your hometown or city	_____° _____	_____° _____
Cairo, Egypt	_____° _____	_____° _____
Sydney, Australia	_____° _____	_____° _____

2. What is located at the following longitudes and latitudes?

   37°E, 55°N _____   87°W, 42°N _____

   33°E, 1°S _____   46°W, 24°S _____

3. The **Torrid Zone** is that part of the Earth where the Sun can be seen straight overhead. The equator is in the middle of the Torrid Zone. The boundaries of the Torrid Zone are called the **Tropic of Cancer** and the **Tropic of Capricorn**. Find the Tropic of Cancer and the Tropic of Capricorn on the map or globe. Describe their locations.

   _____

   _____

   _____

4. Pretend you are flying from the North to the South Pole along the 30° West longitude semicircle. Over which land areas does your flight take you?

   _____

   _____

Math Boxes

1. Estimate the length of this line segment.

about _____ cm

Measure it.   about _____ cm

How far off were you?   about _____ cm

2. Make up a fact triangle.
Write the fact family.

_____ * _____ = _____

_____ * _____ = _____

_____ / _____ = _____

_____ / _____ = _____

3. Insert parentheses to make the number sentences true.

6 + 2 * 4 = 14

6 + 2 * 4 = 32

1 + 8 * 8 + 2 = 90

1 + 8 * 8 + 2 = 67

How to Make a Cut-Away Globe

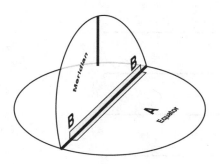

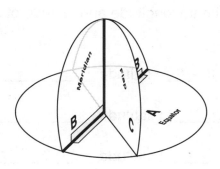

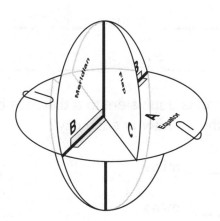

Step 1: Carefully cut out one of the circles A along the dashed lines.

Step 2: Cut out one of the semicircles B and the thin slit on the semicircle.

Step 3: Lay semicircle B on circle A so that the base of the semicircle aligns with the 0° to 180° diameter shown on circle A. Tape the pieces together on both sides of the semicircle. Move the semicircle so that it stands straight up.

Step 4: Cut out one of the semicircles C and cut out the slit. Fold the semicircle in half at the 90° line. Fold it back and forth several times at the same place until you have made a good crease.

Step 5: Slide the slit of semicircle C through the slit of semicircle B.

Step 6: Repeat Steps 1–5 to make a second hemisphere.

Step 7: Put the two hemispheres together with paper clips to make a full globe. Put the 0° labels on circles A together.

Use with Lesson 50.

Locating Places on Atlas Maps

1. Find each of the following cities on the maps in your *World Tour Book*. Record the continent in which it is located.

   a. Lisbon, Portugal
   (on Region 2 map, pp. 22–23)   _____

   b. Bombay, India   _____

   c. Santa Cruz, Bolivia
   (on Region 3 map, pp. 24–25)   _____

   d. Cape Town, South Africa   _____

   e. Seattle, USA   _____

2. Use the maps of continents to find the approximate longitude and latitude of each city.

   a. Lisbon, Portugal   longitude _____ ° *west* ; latitude _____ ° *north*

   b. Bombay, India   longitude _____ ° _____ ; latitude _____ ° _____

   c. Santa Cruz, Bolivia   longitude _____ ° _____ ; latitude _____ ° _____

   d. Cape Town, S. Africa   longitude _____ ° _____ ; latitude _____ ° _____

   e. Seattle, USA   longitude _____ ° _____ ; latitude _____ ° _____

3. A 1-degree interval along a north-south meridian is equivalent to a distance of about 70 miles. About how many miles from the equator is each city?

   a. Lisbon, Portugal   about _____ miles

   b. Bombay, India   about _____ miles

   c. Santa Cruz, Bolivia   about _____ miles

   d. Cape Town, South Africa   about _____ miles

   e. Seattle, USA   about _____ miles

Use with Lesson 51.

The Magnetized Compass*

In ancient times, sailors had only the sun, moon, and stars to aid them in navigation. The most important navigational instrument was the **compass**. The compass was invented more than 1000 years ago. The first compass was a small bar of magnetized iron that was floated on a reed in a bowl of water. The magnet in the iron would make the reed point to the magnetically charged North Pole. Using the compass, sailors could tell in which direction they were going.

You, too, can make a floating compass.

First, magnetize a steel sewing needle by stroking it with one pole of a strong bar magnet. Stroke the needle from end to end. Stroke slowly and gently **in one direction only**. Be sure to lift your hand up in the air before coming down for another stroke.

Slice a round piece ($\frac{1}{2}$-inch thick) from a cork stopper. Cut a groove across the center of the top of the cork. Put the needle in the groove, and place the cork into a glass, china, or aluminum dish filled with water. Add a teaspoon of detergent to lower the surface tension of the water and prevent the cork from moving to one side of the dish and staying there.

The needle will behave like a compass needle. It will assume a North-South position because of the earth's magnetic field.

*Based on an excerpt from *Science for the Elementary School*, 3rd Edition, by Edward Victor.

Use with Lesson 52.

Math Boxes

---

1. Complete the division facts.

$45 \div 9 =$ _____ $24 \div$ _____ $= 6$

$27 \div$ _____ $= 9$ $36 \div 6 =$ _____

$42 \div$ _____ $= 6$ $90 \div 9 =$ _____

---

2. Say the number 4,309,827. What does—

the 3 stand for? _____

the 9 stand for? _____

the 2 stand for? _____

the 4 stand for? _____

---

3. You have 72 cookies. If you pass 8 out to each of your friends until you run out of cookies, how many friends will get cookies?

_____

4. Lunch was served at 11:45 A.M. What time is it 58 minutes later?

_____

Number Tile Problems

Use your number tiles to help you solve these problems.

1. Use odd number tiles only to make the largest possible sum.

2. Use even number tiles (that includes 0) to make the smallest possible sum. Do not use zero as the first digit.

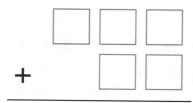

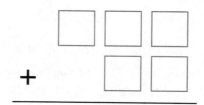

3. Use your five largest number tiles to make the smallest possible difference.

4. Use your five smallest number tiles to make the largest possible difference. Do not use zero as the first digit.

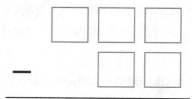

5. Use each of the number tiles 0 to 9 once to find the missing digits in these number sentences.

    a. $7\boxed{} - \boxed{}3 = 36$

    b. $9\boxed{}2 - \boxed{}56 = 82\boxed{}$

    c. $7\boxed{}4 + \boxed{}15 = 1289$

    d. $1\boxed{}4 + 8\boxed{} = \boxed{}14$

Use with Lesson 53.

Fractions and Their Uses

You have been using whole number counting words (one, two, three, ...) since you were quite young. Besides counting words, you may also have used words like "half" in sharing something equally with someone else (half of 6 pieces of candy, half a cookie, or half of a bottle of juice). You learned the symbols 1, 2, 3, ... for the counting words and symbols such as $\frac{1}{2}$ or $\frac{2}{3}$ for fraction words. Later, you learned that besides expressing equal shares, fractions (or decimals) are needed for most measures. Fractions express measurements that come between whole numbers ($4\frac{1}{2}$ miles, $3\frac{5}{8}$ inches, $\frac{2}{3}$ cup).

In *Everyday Mathematics*, you will find fraction notation useful in ways that may be new to you, especially in expressing rates (such as cost per ounce), in making ratio comparisons or calculating percents, or in writing the scale of a map or picture.

Here are a few uses of fractions from some books and newspapers in the office of the authors of this program. Some of these ways of using fractions may be new to you and some may be familiar.

- Some of the ingredients in a recipe for Jambalaya: 3/4 cup rice, 4 ounces each of chicken and of sausage, 4 cups peppers, 7 ounces or 1 2/3 cups chopped onions, 1 1/2 tablespoons chopped thyme, 1/8 teaspoon salt.

- The scale on a map is given as 1:100,000 (another way of expressing $\frac{1}{100,000}$), which means that each inch on the map represents 100,000 inches, or about $1\frac{1}{2}$ miles.

- Over many throws of a 6-sided die, you will probably get each number about one-sixth of the time; that is, the theoretical probability for getting each number is $\frac{1}{6}$. Throwing two dice, the probability of getting 12 is $\frac{1}{36}$ and the probability of getting 7 is $\frac{6}{36}$, or $\frac{1}{6}$.

- A movie critic rated the film *Home Alone* as a $3\frac{1}{2}$-star movie (on a scale of 0 to 4 stars).

- A computer software company's stock listing: close 49 1/2, –1 1/8. Translation: in the last sale of the day, some shares sold for $49.50 each, down 1 1/8 dollars from the previous day.

- One-fifth of the length of a telephone pole should be in the ground.

- On average, about $\frac{1}{16}$ of a person's total weight is skin, about $\frac{2}{5}$ of it is muscle, and about $\frac{1}{12}$ of it is blood.

- Batting averages can be written as fractions with hits in the numerator and "official times at bat" (not including walks, sacrifices, or being hit by a ball) in the denominator, and then converted to three-place decimals.

- In music, marches typically have 4/4 time signatures and waltzes have 3/4 time.

Use with Lesson 54.

Fraction Review

Divide each shape into equal parts. Color a fraction of the parts. Fill in the **whole box**.

1.

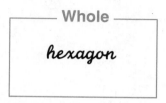

Whole

hexagon

Divide the hexagon into 2 equal parts.
Color $\frac{1}{2}$ of the hexagon.

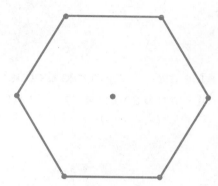

2.

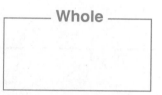

Whole

Divide the hexagon into 3 equal parts.
(**Hint:** Draw 3 rhombuses inside the
hexagon.) Color $\frac{1}{3}$ of the hexagon.

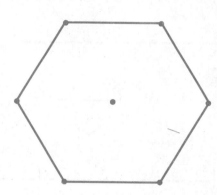

3.

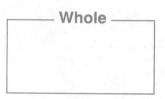

Whole

Divide the rhombus into 2 equal parts.
Color $\frac{0}{2}$ of it.

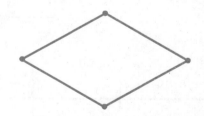

4.

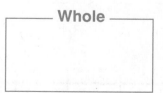

Whole

Divide the trapezoid into 3 equal parts.
Color $\frac{2}{3}$ of the trapezoid.

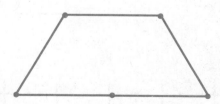

Use with Lesson 54.

Fraction Review (continued)

5.

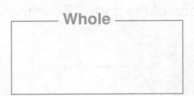

Divide the hexagon into 6 equal parts. Color $\frac{5}{6}$ of the hexagon.

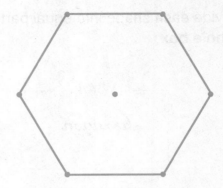

Fill in the missing numbers on the number lines.

6.

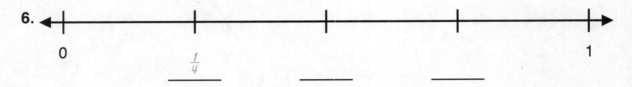

0                    $\frac{1}{4}$ _____   _____   1

7.

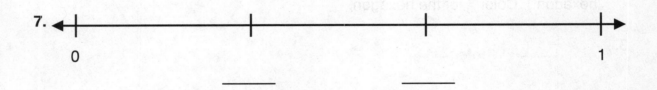

0   _____   _____   1

8.

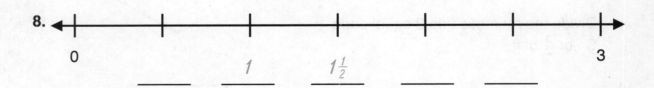

0   _____   _____   1 $1\frac{1}{2}$ _____   _____   3

9.

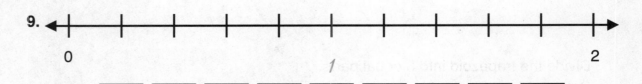

0   1   2

Date _____ Time _____

Math Boxes

1. Solve.

$3 * 40 =$ _____

$90 * 7 =$ _____

$50 * 60 =$ _____

$8 * 200 =$ _____

2. Estimate the size of this angle.

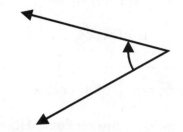

Estimate: about _____ °

Now measure it. about _____ °

3. List the names of the countries on page 32 in your *World Tour Book* whose flags have a circle.

_____

_____

_____

_____

4. In each of the following, write a number that makes the sentence true.

a. $80 /$ _____ > 10

b. $20 *$ _____ < 180

c. $360 /$ _____ > 30

5. Make up a number story for $6 \times 8 = 48$.

_____

_____

_____

_____

_____

Use with Lesson 54.

"Fraction-of" Problems

Solve.

1.

┌─── **Whole** ───┐
│   │
│   *16 nickels* │
│   │
└─────────────────┘

a. Cross out $\frac{1}{4}$ of the nickels.

b. Circle $\frac{3}{4}$ of the nickels. How much

money is that? $_____._____

2.

┌─── **Whole** ───┐
│   │
│   │
│   │
└─────────────────┘

a. Fill in the whole box.

b. Circle $\frac{5}{6}$ of the dimes. How much

money is that? $_____._____

3. Michael has 20 baseball cards. He gives $\frac{1}{5}$ of them to his friend, Alana, and $\frac{2}{5}$ to his brother, Dean.

a. How many baseball cards does he give Alana?   _____ cards

b. How many does he give his brother?   _____ cards

c. How many does he keep for himself?   _____ cards

4. Solve the problems.

┌─── **Whole** ───┐
│   │
│ *bag of marbles*│
│   │
└─────────────────┘

a. $\frac{1}{3}$ of 12 = _____   **b.** $\frac{2}{3}$ of 12 = _____

c. $\frac{3}{5}$ of 15 = _____   **d.** $\frac{3}{4}$ of 36 = _____

e. $\frac{5}{8}$ of 32 = _____   **f.** $\frac{4}{6}$ of 24 = _____   **g.** $\frac{2}{4}$ of 14 = _____

"Fraction-of" Problems (continued)

Luis is staying in a large state park that has 8 hiking trails, some mostly on flat land and others that call for quite a bit of climbing. The trails vary in length and difficulty, as described in the table at the right.

Luis figures that it will take him about 20 minutes to walk 1 mile on an easy trail, about 30 minutes on a moderate trail, and about 40 minutes on a rugged trail.

Trail	Miles	Type
1	$1\frac{1}{4}$	easy
2	2	moderate
3	$\frac{3}{4}$	moderate
4	$1\frac{3}{4}$	rugged
5	$\frac{3}{4}$	rugged
6	$1\frac{1}{2}$	easy
7	$1\frac{1}{2}$	moderate
8	$3\frac{1}{2}$	moderate

5. About how long will it take him to walk the following trails?

   a. Trail 2: about _____ minutes   b. Trail 5: about _____ minutes

   c. Trail 6: about _____ minutes   d. Trail 4: about _____ minutes

6. If Luis wants to hike for about $\frac{3}{4}$ of an hour, which trail should he choose?

   _____

7. If he wants to hike for about 25 minutes, which trail should he choose?

   _____

8. About how long would it take him to complete Trail 3?

   about _____ minutes

9. Do you think Luis could walk Trail 8 in under 2 hours? _____ Explain.

_____

_____

_____

_____

Use with Lesson 55.

Math Boxes

---

1. Estimate the dimensions of this page.

About _____ cm long

About _____ cm wide

2. You start with a number. Double it. Triple the answer. You get 60. With what number did you start?

_____

3. Solve.

$45 ÷$ _____ $= 9$

$450 ÷$ _____ $= 9$

$450 /$ _____ $= 50$

$50 * 90 =$ _____

$500 *$ _____ $= 4500$

4. Tom was facing north. He turned to his left (counterclockwise) until he was facing east. How many degrees did he turn?

_____

💡 Animal Groups

You have heard of a pride of lions. Did you know about—

- a murder of crows
- a skulk of foxes
- a peep of chickens
- a crash of rhinos
- a siege of herons
- a parliament of owls

Source: Wallechinsky, David, Irving Wallace, and Amy Wallace. *The Book of Lists*. New York: Bantam Books, 1977.

Use with Lesson 55.

Pattern-Block Fractions

For Problems 1–6, Shape A is the whole.

1. Cover Shape A on Activity Sheet 2 with trapezoid blocks. What fraction of the shape is covered by 1 trapezoid?

    _____

2. Cover Shape A with rhombuses. What fraction of the shape is covered—

    By 1 rhombus?   _____

    By 2 rhombuses?   _____

3. Cover Shape A with triangles. What fraction of the shape is covered—

    By 1 triangle?   _____

    By 3 triangles?   _____

    By 5 triangles?   _____

4. Cover Shape A with 1 trapezoid and 3 triangles. With a straightedge, draw the result on the hexagon at the right. Label each part with a fraction.

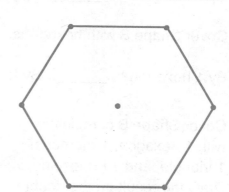

5. Cover Shape A with 2 rhombuses and 2 triangles. Draw the result on the hexagon below. Label each part with a fraction.

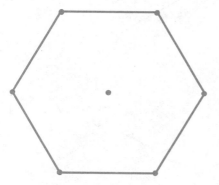

6. Cover Shape A with 1 trapezoid, 1 rhombus, and 1 triangle. Draw the result on the hexagon below. Label each part with a fraction.

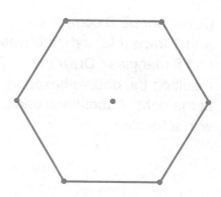

Pattern-Block Fractions (continued)

For Problems 7–12, Shape B is the whole.

> **Whole**
> Shape B –
> double hexagon

7. Cover Shape B with trapezoids. What fraction of the shape is covered—

   By 1 trapezoid? _____   By 2 trapezoids? _____   By 3 trapezoids? _____

8. Cover Shape B with rhombuses. What fraction of the shape is covered—

   By 1 rhombus? _____   By 3 rhombuses? _____   By 5 rhombuses? _____

9. Cover Shape B with triangles. What fraction of the shape is covered—

   By 1 triangle? _____   By 2 triangles? _____   By 3 triangles? _____

10. Cover Shape B with hexagons. What fraction of the shape is covered—

    By 1 hexagon? _____   By 2 hexagons? _____

11. Cover Shape B completely
    with 1 hexagon, 1 rhombus,
    1 triangle, and 1 trapezoid.
    Draw the result on the double
    hexagon at the right. Label
    each part with a fraction.

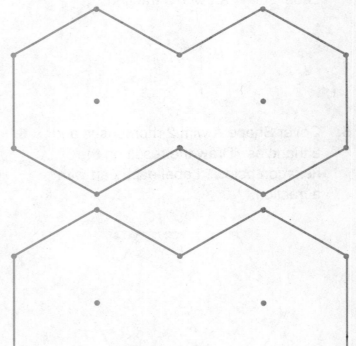

12. Cover Shape B completely
    with 1 trapezoid, 2 rhombuses,
    and 5 triangles. Draw the
    result on the double hexagon
    at the right. Label each part
    with a fraction.

Use with Lesson 56.

Pattern-Block Fractions (continued)

For Problems 13–16, Shape C is the whole.

13. Cover Shape C with trapezoids. What fraction of the shape is covered—

By 1 trapezoid? _____   By 2 trapezoids? _____   By 6 trapezoids? _____

14. Cover Shape C with rhombuses. What fraction of the shape is covered—

By 1 rhombus? _____   By 3 rhombuses? _____   By 6 rhombuses? _____

15. Cover Shape C with triangles. What fraction of the shape is covered—

By 1 triangle? _____   By 3 triangles? _____   By 12 triangles? _____

16. Cover Shape C completely, using one or more of each of the trapezoids, rhombuses, triangles, and hexagons. Draw the result on the big hexagon below. Label each part with a fraction.

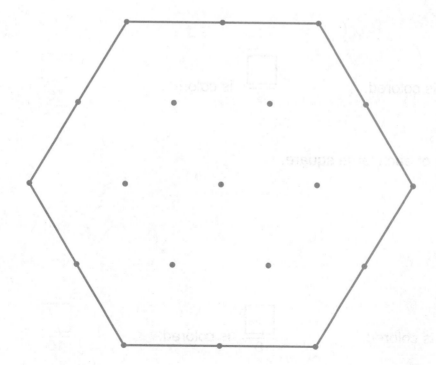

Many Names for Fractions

Color the squares and write the missing numerators.

1. Color $\frac{1}{2}$ of each large square.

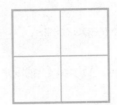   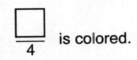   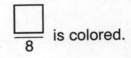

$\frac{1}{2}$ of the square is colored. $\frac{}{4}$ is colored. $\frac{}{8}$ is colored.

2. Color $\frac{1}{4}$ of each large square.

   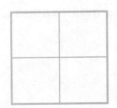   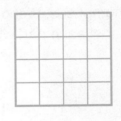

$\frac{}{4}$ is colored. $\frac{}{8}$ is colored. $\frac{}{16}$ is colored.

3. Color $\frac{3}{4}$ of each large square.

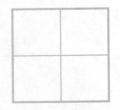      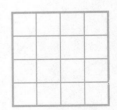

$\frac{}{4}$ is colored. $\frac{}{8}$ is colored. $\frac{}{16}$ is colored.

Math Boxes

1. Circle the values below that would fall between the two given numbers on the number line given below.

    11.00   10.85   10.01   11.10   10.00

    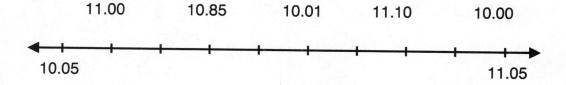

    10.05   11.05

    Name one other value that could
    be found on the number line.   _____

2. Write a numeral that has a 7 in the ten thousands place, a 2 in the millions place and a 5 in the tens place. Also the numeral must be even and have at least one 0.

    _____

    Read your numeral to a partner.

3.

```
   145          290
 +  36        + 136
```


```
   201         2001
 -   2        -  12
```

4. a. Draw a 90° angle.   b. Draw a 45° angle.

Math Boxes

---

1. If you have 72 gallons of water in a tank and you remove 9 gallons a day, how long will it take to empty the tank?

_____

2. Solve.

200 * _____ = 1000

40 * _____ = 2000

9 * _____ = 18,000

60 * 700 = _____

3. When asked how many glasses of milk they drank in a week, 10 students responded as follows: 16, 13, 15, 20, 8, 10, 15, 12, 10, 18.

Find the range: _____

Find the median: _____

🔆 Flea Jumping

A flea can jump 25 centimeters high, or about 10 inches. That is 60 times its own body length. If a person could jump 60 times her own height, she could easily hop over a 365-foot building. That's almost $\frac{1}{3}$ the height of the Empire State Building.

Source: Houwink, R. *Did You Know?* Mahwah, New Jersey: Watermill Press, 1989.

Date _____ Time _____

Math Message

Quinn, Nancy, Diego, Paula, and Kiana were given 4 chocolate bars to share. All 4 bars were the same size.

1. Quinn and Nancy shared a chocolate bar. Quinn ate $\frac{1}{4}$ of the bar and Nancy ate $\frac{2}{4}$.

    Who ate more?   _____

    How much of the bar was left?   _____

2. Diego, Paula, and Kiana each ate part of one of the other chocolate bars. Diego ate $\frac{2}{3}$ of a bar, Paula $\frac{2}{5}$ of a bar, and Kiana $\frac{5}{6}$ of a bar.

    Who ate more, Diego or Paula?   _____

    Diego or Kiana?   _____

    Nancy or Diego?   _____

Be ready to defend your answers.

Rules for *Fraction Top-It*

Materials: a set of fraction cards

Number of players: 2–4

Directions:

Deal the same number of cards, fraction-side up, to each player:

*   16 cards each, if there are 2 players;
*   10 cards each, if there are 3 players; and
*   8 cards each, if there are 4 players.

Place the cards on the playing surface in front of each player, fraction-side up.

Starting with the dealer and going in a clockwise direction, each player plays a card. The player with the largest fraction wins the round and takes the cards. If there is a tie for the largest fraction, each player plays another card. The player with the largest fraction takes all the cards. Players may check who has the largest fraction by turning over the cards and comparing the amount shaded.

The player who took the cards starts the next round. The game is over when all cards have been played. The player who took the most cards wins.

Use with Lesson 59.

Math Boxes

1. If you were facing north and wanted to be facing west, you would turn—

_____° clockwise

or

_____° counterclockwise

2. Shade more than 0.02 and less than 0.1 of the grid.

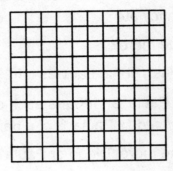

3. Use your template to make a regular hexagon. Measure one of the angles with your protractor. _____°

Fractions and Decimals

┌─ Whole ─┐
large square

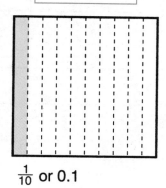

$\frac{1}{10}$ or 0.1

1.

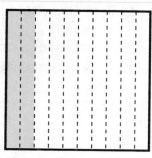

$\frac{2}{10}$ of the square is shaded.

$\frac{2}{10}$ = 0._____

2.

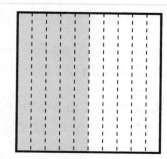

$\frac{1}{2}$ is shaded.

How many tenths? _____

$\frac{1}{2}$ = $\frac{\square}{10}$ = 0._____

3.

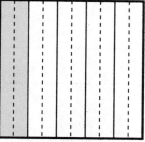

$\frac{1}{5}$ is shaded.

How many tenths? _____

$\frac{1}{5}$ = $\frac{\square}{10}$ = 0._____

4.

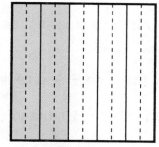

$\frac{2}{5}$ is shaded.

How many tenths? _____

$\frac{2}{5}$ = $\frac{\square}{10}$ = 0._____

5. $\frac{3}{5}$ = $\frac{\square}{10}$ = 0._____

6. $\frac{4}{5}$ = $\frac{\square}{10}$ = 0._____

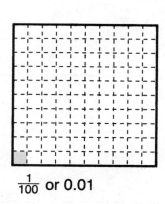

$\frac{1}{100}$ or 0.01

7.

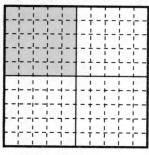

$\frac{1}{4}$ is shaded.

$\frac{1}{4}$ = $\frac{\square}{100}$ = 0._____

8.

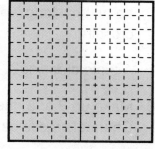

$\frac{3}{4}$ is shaded.

$\frac{3}{4}$ = $\frac{\square}{100}$ = 0._____

Use with Lesson 60.

English Channel Crossings

Read pages 8 and 9 in your *World Tour Book* before you answer the questions.

1. In 1965, Ted Erikson set a world record for a double crossing of the English Channel. What was his time? _____

2. Who is the world record holder for a double crossing of the Channel, as of 1994? _____

   What was his time? _____

3. How much less is this time than Ted Erikson's time? _____

4. In 1981, Jon Erikson completed the first triple crossing. What was his time? _____

5. What is the world record for a triple crossing, as of 1994? _____

   How much less is this time than Jon Erikson's time? _____

6. About how long did it take Ted's dog Umbra to swim 2.4 miles? _____

   If Umbra could keep up that pace, estimate about how long it would take her to swim 10 miles. _____

7. Penny Dean holds the world record for a single crossing, as of 1994. If she could keep up her world record pace, about how long would it take her to complete a double crossing? _____

   A triple crossing? _____

8. Make up 2 or 3 questions, using information about Channel crossings.

   _____

   _____

   _____

Math Boxes

---

1. If you turned this page 270° counterclockwise, which Math Box would be on the left?

   _____

---

2. Complete.

   40 * 50 = _____   _____ * 9 = 7200

   70 * 300 = _____   90 * _____ = 810

   60 * _____ = 180   60 * _____ = 3600

---

3. Name three properties of a polygon.

   a. _____

   b. _____

   c. _____

   Draw a polygon.

Making Spinners

1. Make a spinner. Color the circle in 6 different colors so that the paper clip has the **same chance** of landing on each of the colors.

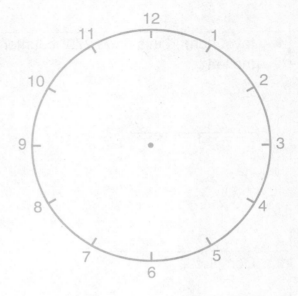

2. Make another spinner. Color the circle red, blue, and green so that the paper clip has—

   • a $\frac{1}{6}$ chance of landing on red

   and

   • a $\frac{1}{3}$ chance of landing on blue.

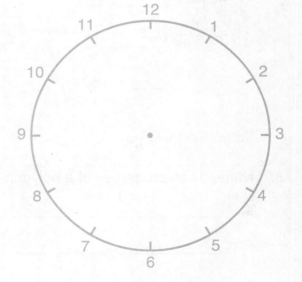

   a. What fraction of the circle did you color—

   red _____   blue _____   green _____

   b. Suppose you spun the paper clip 24 times. About how many times would you expect it to land on—

   red _____   blue _____   green _____

   c. Suppose you spun the paper clip 90 times. About how many times would you expect it to land on—

   red _____   blue _____   green _____

A Coin-Drop Experiment

To do this experiment, you will need to color the 100-grid on Activity Sheet 4. Color the small squares on your 100-grid as follows:

Color	Black	Red	Blue	Green	White
Number of squares	1	4	10	35	50

You may color them in any way you want. The colors may form a pattern or a picture, or they may be completely without a plan.

How To Do the Experiment

Place the 100-grid on the floor. Hold a penny or dime about waist high above the grid and let it drop on the grid **without aiming**. Record the color of the square on which the coin lands.

- If the coin does not land on the mat, it does not count.

- If the coin lands on more than one color, record the color that is covered by most of the coin. If you can't tell, the toss does not count.

Predict the Outcome of the Experiment

On which color is the coin most likely to land? _____

On which color is it least likely to land? _____

Suppose you dropped the coin 100 times. How many times would you expect it to land on each of the colors? Record your predictions in the following table.

Predictions of Results of 100 Coin-Drops

	Black	Red	Blue	Green	White
Number of squares	1	4	10	35	50
Fraction of times coin will land on color	$\frac{1}{100}$				
Prediction: Percent of times coin will land on color	_1_%	____%	____%	____%	____%

Use with Lessons 63 and 64.

A Coin-Drop Experiment (continued)

Do the Experiment

For this experiment, you and your partner will each drop a penny or dime on your own 100-grid 50 times. Take turns: one partner drops the coin 50 times, the other tallies the results in a chart, like the one at the right. After 50 drops, trade roles.

When you have finished—

1. Record the results of your 50 drops in the table below.

2. Also record the results in the table below your 100-grid on Activity Sheet 4.

3. Cut off the table on Activity Sheet 4 and give it to your teacher.

4. Fill out the percent row in the table below. For example, if your coin landed on blue 15 times out of 50 drops, this is the same as landing 30 times out of 100 drops, or 30% of the time.

Tally of Coin-Drops
Black
Red
Blue
Green
White

My Results for 50 Coin-Drops

	Black	Red	Blue	Green	White	Total
Number of times coin landed on color						
Percent of times coin landed on color	____%	____%	____%	____%	____%	____%

5. Record the class totals in the table below.

Class Results for 1000 Coin-Drops

	Black	Red	Blue	Green	White	Total
Number of times coin landed on color						
Percent of times coin landed on color	____%	____%	____%	____%	____%	____%

Use with Lessons 63 and 64.

Math Boxes

1. Fill in the missing numbers.

$4 * \underline{\hspace{2cm}} = 32$

$5 * \underline{\hspace{2cm}} = 75$

$64 = 8 * \underline{\hspace{2cm}}$

$4 = \underline{\hspace{2cm}} / 6$

$27 = 3 * \underline{\hspace{2cm}}$

2. The following numbers came up when Tina threw two dice:
4, 1, 9, 6, 12, 12, 2, 1, 6, 12, 3

What is the median? _____

Mode? _____

Maximum? _____

Minimum? _____

Range? _____

3. Write a number story for the number model $15 \div 3 = 5$.

_____

_____

_____

_____

_____

_____

4. Make 5000's.

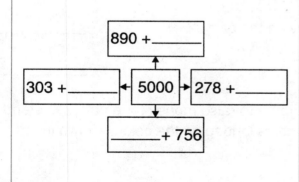

5. The late bus arrives at 3:20 P.M. It is 2:57 P.M. How many minutes before the bus will arrive?

_____

A Carnival Game

1. Imagine that your class is
   using the class quilt for a
   carnival game. The quilt is
   placed on the floor as a
   target mat for coin-tossing.
   The player stands about
   5 feet from the target mat
   and tosses a coin. The rules
   are the same as before: If
   the coin does not land on a
   color, the player gets another
   turn. The player may win a
   prize, depending on the color
   the coin lands on. A player
   must buy a ticket for 10 cents to play.

   Suppose that you bought 50 tickets.

   a. How much would you pay for 50 tickets?   _____

      Suppose that your 50 tosses landed on the colors shown in the table in
      Part 4 on page 136.

   b. How much prize money would you have won?   _____

   c. Would you have won or lost money on the game?   _____

      How much?   _____

2. Suppose the class decided to use the game to raise money for a party. Pretend
   that they sell 1000 tickets and that the coins landed on the colors shown in
   Part 5 on page 136.

   a. How much would the class collect on the sale of tickets? _____

   b. How much prize money would the class have to pay?   _____

   c. How much money would the class have raised?   _____

Use with Lesson 64.

A Carnival Game (continued)

Project

3. You and your classmates make up your own carnival game.

a. Record how much you would charge for a ticket and what the prizes would be for each color.

Ticket Price
_____ per toss

Prizes	
black	_____
red	_____
blue	_____
green	_____
white	_____

b. Use the results in Part 5 on page 136 to answer the questions.

Would the class have won or lost money? _____

How much? _____

4. Suppose the class ran your game on Parents' Night.

a. How many tickets do you estimate the class would sell? _____

b. How much money would the class get from ticket sales? _____

c. About how much money should you expect to pay in prizes? _____

d. About how much money should the class expect to earn? _____

Use with Lesson 64.

Glossary

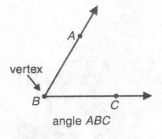

vertex

angle *ABC*

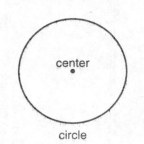

bar graph

circle

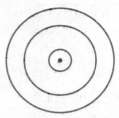

concave polygons

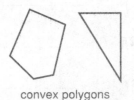

concentric circles

convex polygons

acute angle An angle that measures less than 90°.

angle A figure consisting of two *rays* with the same *endpoint*.

bank balance The amount of money in a bank account at a given time.

bar graph A graph that uses horizontal or vertical bars to represent data.

base-ten system A system for writing numbers based on groupings in tens, hundreds, thousands, and so on.

center of a circle A point that is the same distance from all points on a circle.

centimeter (cm) In the metric system, a unit of length defined as $\frac{1}{100}$ of a meter; equal to 10 millimeters, or $\frac{1}{10}$ of a decimeter.

circle The set of all points in a plane that are the same distance from a given point (the *center* of the circle).

circumference The distance around a circle.

clockwise rotation A rotation in the direction of the rotation of the hands of a clock.

concave polygon A polygon in which at least one vertex is "pushed in." Also called *nonconvex*.

concentric circles Circles that have the same center.

convex polygon A polygon in which all vertices are "pushed out."

counterclockwise rotation A rotation in the opposite direction of the rotation of the hands of a clock.

data Numerical and other factual information that may be derived from scientific experiments, surveys, or in other ways that rely on observation, questioning, and measurement.

degree (°) A unit of measure for angles; based on dividing a circle into 360 equal parts.

denominator The number of equal parts into which the whole (the unit or the ONE) is divided. In the fraction $\frac{a}{b}$, b is the denominator.

deposit An amount of money, put into a bank account, that is added to the *bank balance*.

diameter A line segment that passes through the center of a circle or sphere and has its endpoints on the circle or sphere; also, the length of such a segment.

digit In our base-ten numeration system, one of the symbols 0, 1, 2, 3, 4, 5, 6, 7, 8, 9. For example, the numeral 145 is made up of the digits 1, 4, and 5.

endpoint The point at either end of a line segment; also, the point at the beginning of a ray. A line segment is named by its endpoints: "Segment *LT*" or "segment *TL*" is the line segment between (and including) points *L* and *T*.

equally likely Events that have the same chance of occurring.

equilateral triangle A triangle with all three sides the same length.

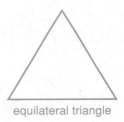

equilateral triangle

equivalent fractions Fractions that name the same number.

estimate A "rough" calculation; not exact.

extended multiplication fact A product of tens, hundreds, thousands, and so on, in which all but the first digit of each factor are zeros (for example, 6 * 70, 60 * 7, 60 * 70).

fact family A group of related multiplication and division facts: 6 * 7 = 42, 7 * 6 = 42, 42/6 = 7, 42/7 = 6.

factor A number that is being multiplied. In 4 * 3 = 12, 4 and 3 are factors.

hemisphere One half of a sphere.

heptagon A polygon with seven sides.

hexagon A polygon with six sides.

hexagram A six-pointed star formed by extending the sides of a regular hexagon.

hexagram

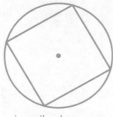

inscribed square

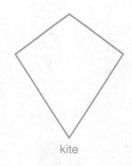

kite

line plot

line segment *AB*

inscribed polygon A polygon whose vertices are points on a circle or other figure.

interest An amount earned for the use of money deposited in a savings account. The *rate of interest* (usually given as a percent naming cents per dollar) is used to calculate the amount of interest earned.

intersect To meet.

kite A quadrilateral with two pairs of adjacent equal sides.

landmarks Measures, used to describe a set of data, including *median*, *mean*, *mode*, *maximum*, *minimum*, and *range*.

latitude The measure of an angle, whose vertex is the center of the earth, used to indicate the location of a place with reference to the equator.

line (straight line) A geometric figure that can be thought of as a line segment that extends in both directions without end.

line plot A "rough" graph used to display the number of times each value in a set of data occurs.

line segment A geometric figure that represents the shortest path between two points, called the *endpoints* of the segment.

longitude The measure of an angle, whose vertex is the center of the earth, used to indicate the location of a place with reference to the prime meridian.

map scale The ratio of distances on a map or globe to the actual distances.

maximum The greatest value in a set of data.

median The middle value in a set of data, listed in order from smallest to largest (or largest to smallest).

minimum The smallest value in a set of data.

mode The value or category that occurs most often in a set of data.

multiplication fact The product of two numbers, each a number from 0 through 10.

nonconvex *See concave.*

number model A number sentence used to represent the relationship between quantities in a number story.

number sentence A sentence that is either true or false, made up of numerals, operation symbols (+, −, *, /), and relation symbols (=, <, >).

numerator In a whole divided into a number of equal parts, the number of equal parts being considered. In the fraction $\frac{a}{b}$, *a* is the numerator.

obtuse angle An angle that measures more than 90° and less than 180°.

obtuse angle

octagon A polygon with eight sides.

open sentence A number sentence in which missing numbers are represented by letters or other symbols.

ordered pair Two numbers, given in a specific order, used to identify points on a coordinate grid. (For example, (2,3).)

parallel lines (segments, rays) Lines (segments, rays) that are the same distance apart and never meet, no matter how far they are extended.

parallelogram A quadrilateral in which pairs of opposite sides are parallel.

parallelogram

pentagon A polygon with five sides.

polygon A two-dimensional figure consisting of line segments (*sides*) in which each vertex is the endpoint of two line segments and the number of sides is equal to the number of vertices. The *interior* of a polygon consists of all the points of the plane "inside" the polygon.

polygon with interior shaded

product The result of multiplying two numbers, called *factors*. For example, in 4 * 3 = 12, 12 is the product.

quadrangle (quadrilateral) A polygon with four sides.

range The difference between the maximum and minimum in a set of data.

rate of interest *See interest.*

ray A geometric figure that can be thought of as a line segment that extends in one direction without end.

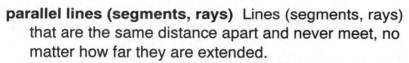

ray *AB*

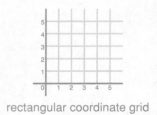

rectangular coordinate grid

reflex angle

regular hexagon

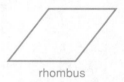

rhombus

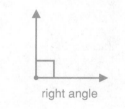

right angle

straight angle

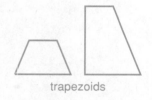

trapezoids

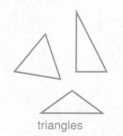

triangles

rectangle A parallelogram whose angles are all right angles.

rectangular coordinate grid A grid formed by two number lines that intersect at right angles at their 0 points.

reflex angle An angle that measures more than 180°.

regular polygon A convex polygon in which all sides are the same length and all angles are the same size.

rhombus A parallelogram whose sides are all the same length.

right angle An angle that measures 90°.

rotation A turn about a center point or axis.

side Any one of the line segments that make up a polygon.

solution of an open sentence The number used to replace the *variable* to make a true sentence.

square A rectangle whose sides are all the same length.

square number A product of a whole number multiplied by itself. For example, 25 is a square number, because 25 = 5 * 5.

straight angle An angle that measures 180°.

tally chart A table that displays each occurrence of a piece of data with a tally mark.

trapezoid A quadrilateral with exactly one pair of parallel sides.

triangle A polygon with three sides and three angles.

turn A rotation.

turn-around facts Two multiplication facts whose factors and products are the same. (The factors are in a different order.)

variable The letter or symbol that represents a missing number in an open sentence.

vertex The point at which the rays of an angle or two sides of a polygon meet.

vertices Plural of *vertex*.

Measuring Angles with a 360° Angle Measurer

The circle at the bottom of the page can be used to measure angles.

Cut out the angle measurer very carefully around the circular edge. Punch a hole in the center of the circle with your pencil point.

Here is how to use the angle measurer to measure angle *A* at the right.

Step 1: Put the hole at the center of the measurer over the vertex of the angle.

Step 2: Line up the 0° mark with the side of the angle so that you can measure the angle clockwise. Make sure that the hole stays over the vertex.

Step 3: Read the degree measure at the mark on the measurer that lines up with the second side of the angle. This is the measure of the angle.

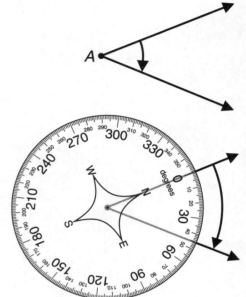

1.   What is the measure of angle *A*?

     about _____ °

2.   Use your angle measurer to
     measure angle *B*.

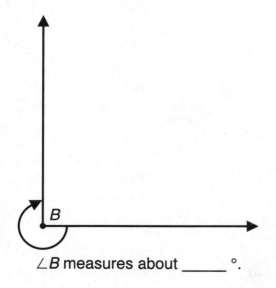

∠*B* measures about _____ °.

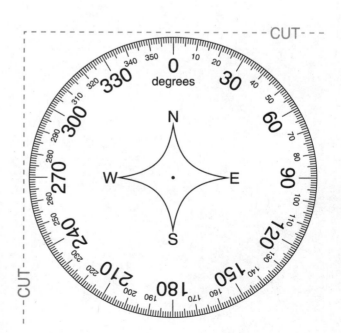

Activity Sheet 1

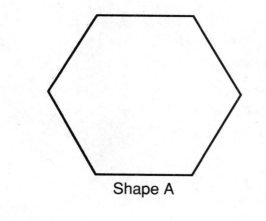

Shape A

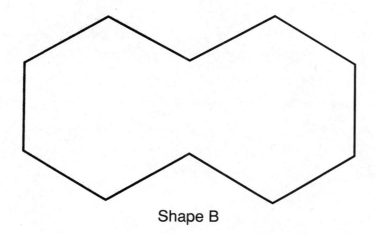

Shape B

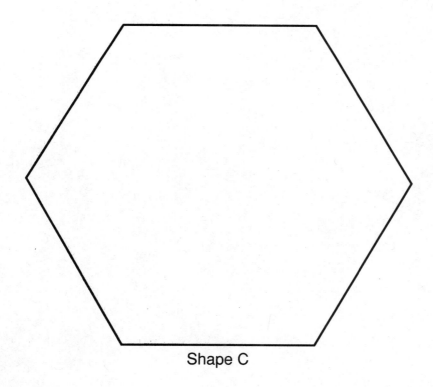

Shape C

Spinner Experiments

1. Use a paper clip and pencil to make a spinner.

    a. Spin the paper clip 4 times. Record
        the number of times it lands on the
        shaded part and on the white part.

shaded	white

    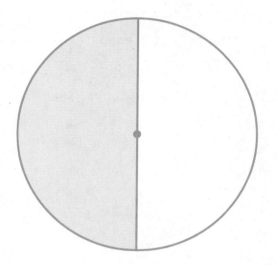

    b. Record the number of times the
        paper clip lands on the shaded part
        and on the white part **for the whole
        class**.

shaded	white

2. Make another spinner. Color the circle blue and red so that the paper clip is
    twice as likely to land on blue as on red.

    a. Spin the paper clip 4 times.
        Record the number of times it
        lands on blue and on red.

blue	red

    b. Record the number of times the
        paper clip lands on blue and on
        red **for the whole class**.

blue	red

3. What would you expect after spinning the paper clip 300 times?

blue	red

Activity Sheet 3

My Results for 50 Coin-Drops

	Black	Red	Blue	Green	White	Total
Number of times coin landed on color						

Activity Sheet 4

*, / **Fact Triangles 1**

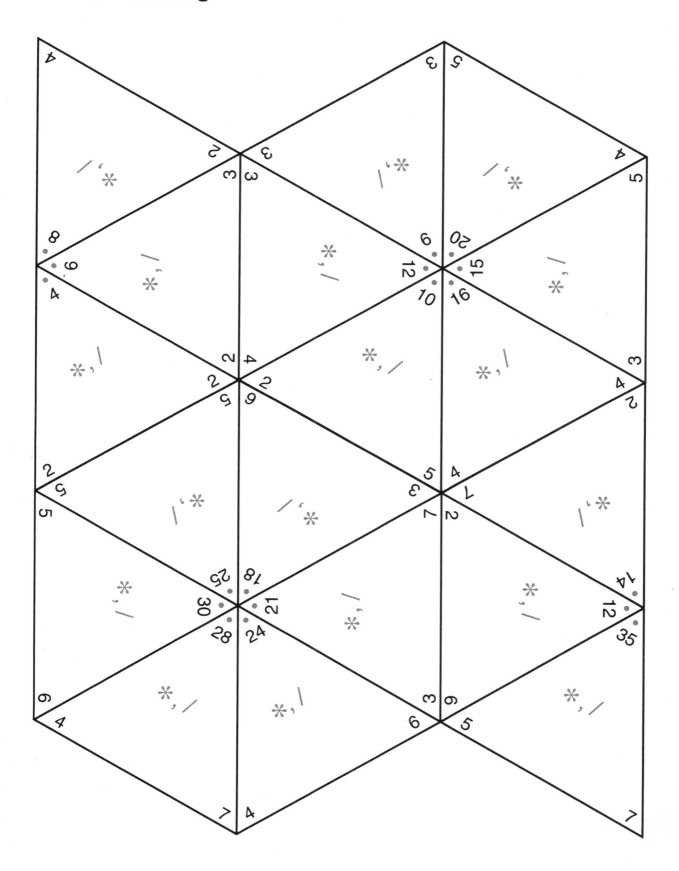

*, / Fact Triangles 2

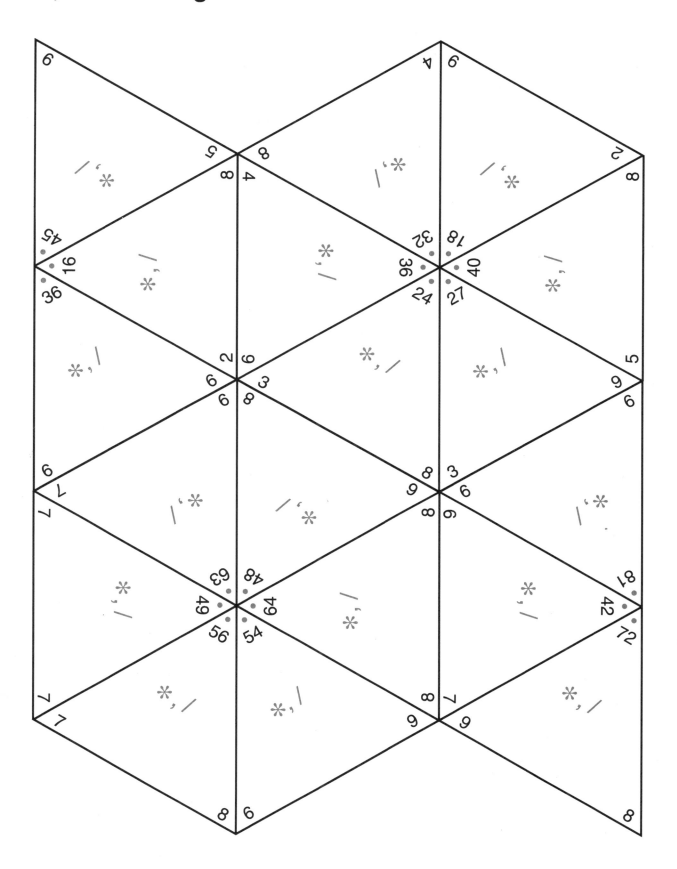

Use with Lesson 19.

Activity Sheet 6

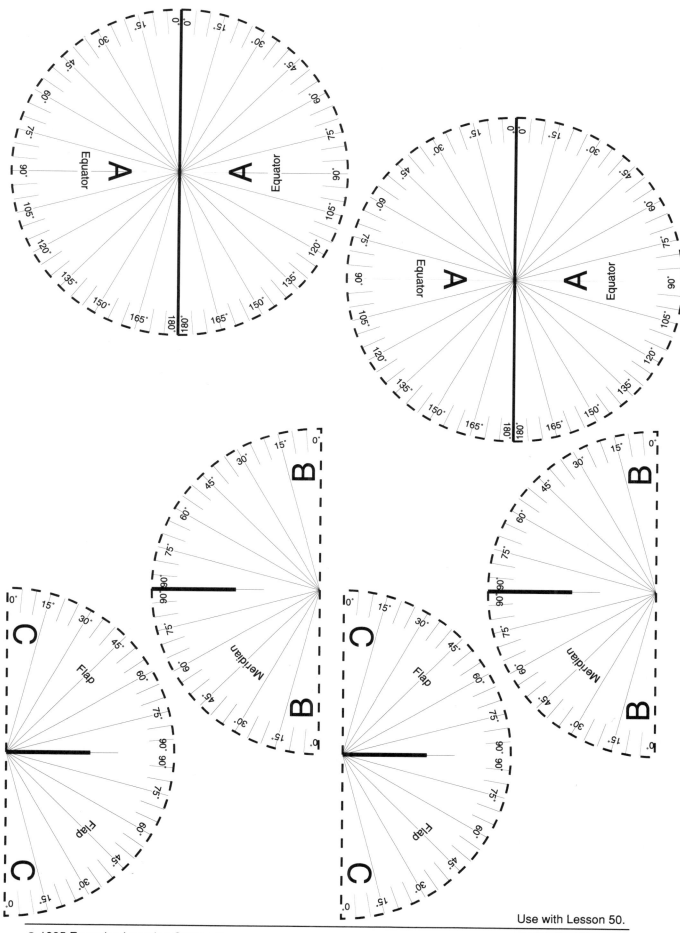

Use with Lesson 50.

Activity Sheet 7

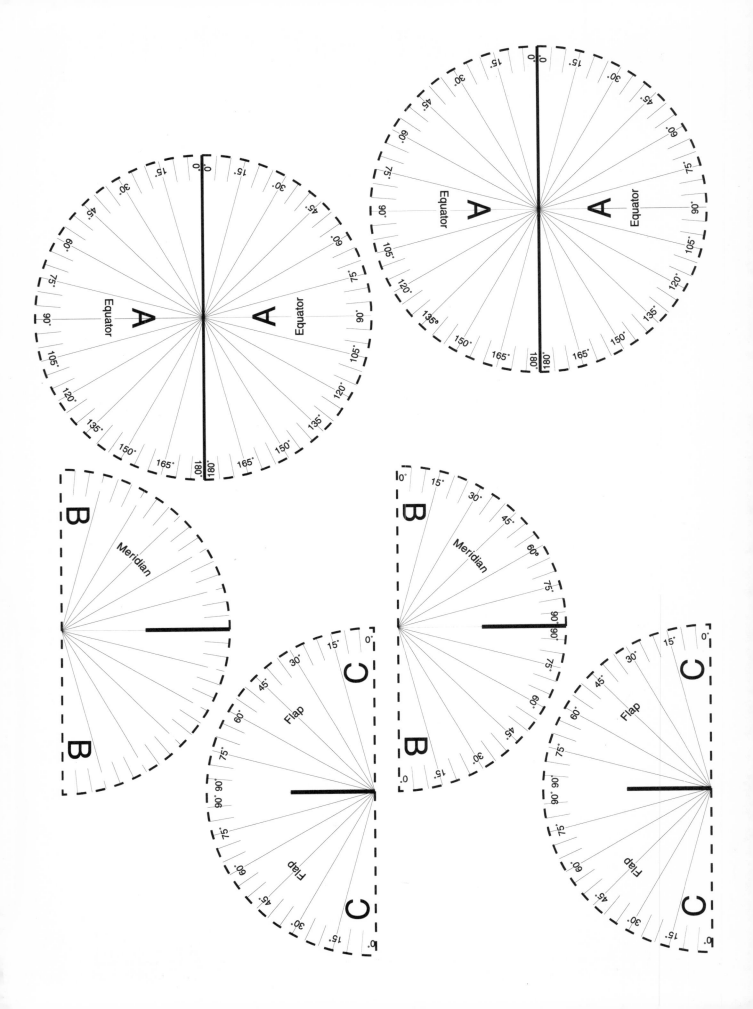

Fraction Cards 1

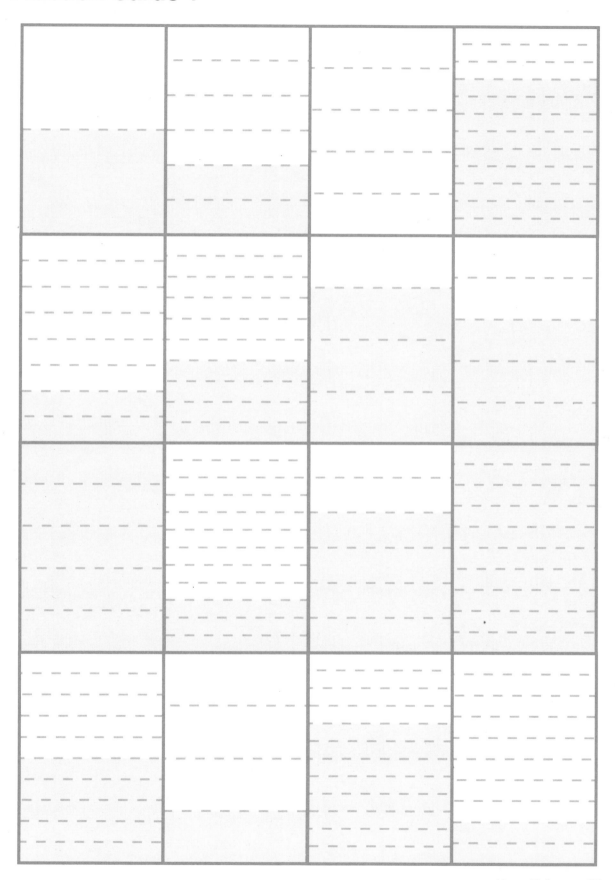

Use with Lesson 57.

Activity Sheet 8

$\dfrac{9}{}$	$\dfrac{}{5}$	$\dfrac{2}{}$	$\dfrac{}{2}$
$\dfrac{3}{}$	$\dfrac{}{4}$	$\dfrac{4}{}$	$\dfrac{2}{}$
$\dfrac{10}{}$	$\dfrac{}{6}$	$\dfrac{3}{}$	$\dfrac{}{5}$
$\dfrac{2}{}$	$\dfrac{}{12}$	$\dfrac{1}{}$	$\dfrac{}{10}$

Fraction Cards 2

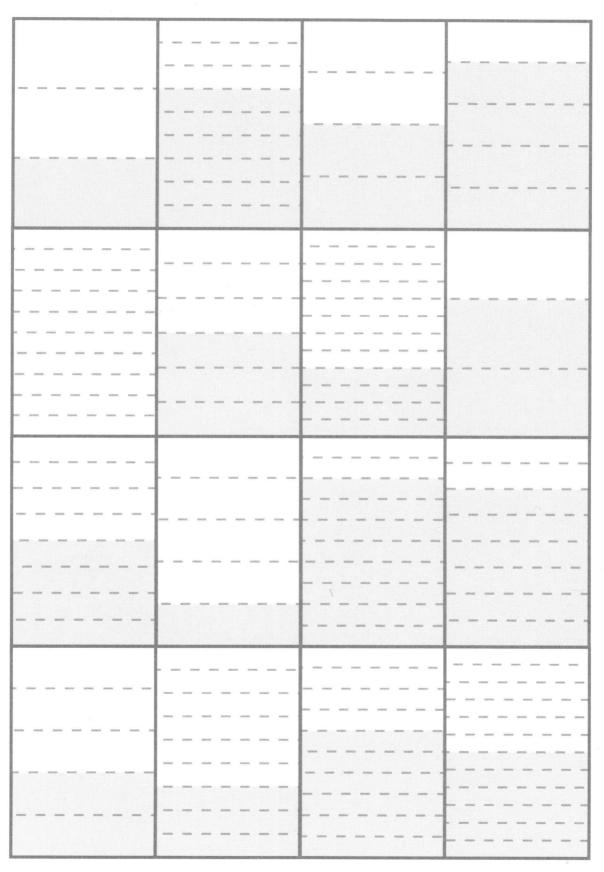

Use with Lesson 57.

Activity Sheet 9

$\dfrac{}{5}$	$\dfrac{2}{}$	$\dfrac{}{9}$	$\dfrac{1}{}$
$\dfrac{}{3}$	$\dfrac{4}{}$	$\dfrac{3}{}$	$\dfrac{0}{}$
$\dfrac{6}{}$	$\dfrac{}{10}$	$\dfrac{1}{}$	$\dfrac{}{8}$
$\dfrac{}{12}$	$\dfrac{6}{}$	$\dfrac{}{9}$	$\dfrac{2}{}$

Computation Tiles

0	1	2	3	4
0	1	2	3	4
5	6	7	8	9
5	6	7	8	9
+	−	*	/	=
+	−	×	÷	=

Activity Sheet 10